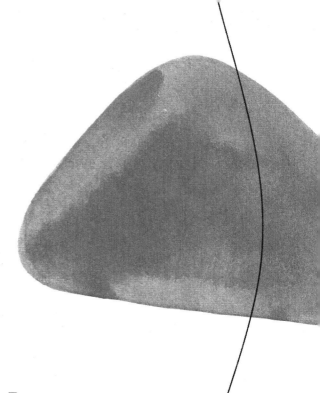

DEATH IS NO EXCUSE

Planning for Death, Disability,
Divorce and Other Disasters

DAVID BAKER

℗ 2021, End of Vandalism Books; End of Vandalism Books is an Imprint of Jay-Hey
Publishers

ISBN: 978-1-66780-314-2

TABLE OF CONTENTS

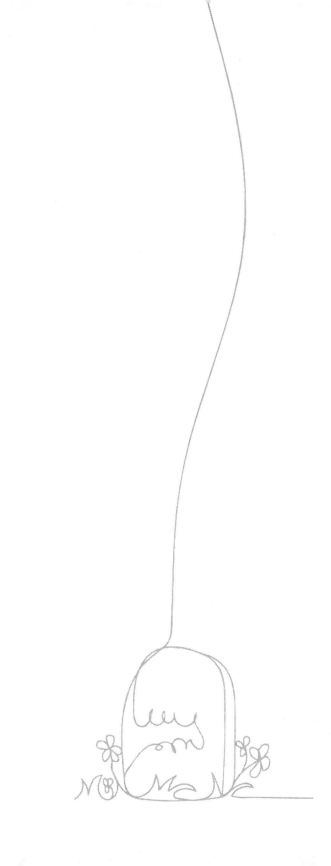

1. YOU'RE GONNA DIE

If I got a hundred dollars for every time I heard somebody say, "Here's what happens *if* I die....," I could've retired, a long time ago.

It's *when* you die, and no, it doesn't matter if you're a big shot or just a medium shot—you're still gonna die.

I'm a probate lawyer. I do wills, plan for death and disability and clean up what's left when people die. If my job has taught me anything over the past forty years, it's that life's a sucker bet: Something's trying to kill you, every stinking minute of every single day.

Don't get me started on roofers, tuck-pointers, circus performers or guys who feed tree branches into those buzzing mulching machines. The thing is, though, they all have reason to expect to get dropped, crunched or pulverized by the jaws of fate. But then, there's this:

I was once involved in reporting a case where a woman standing on a street corner was struck and killed by a falling stone gargoyle. The building ornament had been loosened from the crumbling skyscraper's outer wall through a series of seemingly random events. A dental hygienist in an office with a window ledge above the gargoyle, started a small window-box garden. Dripping water from her garden seeped into the foundation holding the sculpted critter, although that alone would not have been enough to dislodge the gargoyle. Turns out, fertilizer and bird droppings from sparrows and pigeons feeding on the seeds in her garden laced the dripping water, so that corrosive mixture set loose the crashing sculpture.

If random, unavoidable death weren't bad enough, there's the people who get fair warning: I know this accountant who was in a plane that crash landed on a runway, surrounded by fire trucks. He survived the crash, as did the rest of the passengers, but before he jumped on the escape chute he went back up the aisle for his carry-on, flight attendants screaming at him all the way. He barely made it off in time. When I asked what was in his bag, he admitted it was just dirty laundry, a pair of gym shoes and a half-eaten sack lunch.

Then there's the phenomena of people with money and power, who take crazy risks because they think that with their stature comes a suspension of the basic laws of physics. Private airplane pilots are some of the worst: I recall one such crash victim who had multiple funerals over the years, as picnickers located his assorted body parts, spread around in different rural hamlets.

These last two folks are *Death Deniers*—grown adults who nonetheless think they're never going to die.

People like this are my biggest headache. Not just because they're pretty silly—they're all gonna die—but because there's a symptom that comes with this phenomenon, an attitude I call, "God will balance my checkbook." Put another way, Americans generally don't do anything to plan for death, and as a consequence, their loved ones need to deal with their screwed-up estates after they're gone. Me, I need to charge legal fees to their estates for mopping up these messes, and the families hate it. As one disgruntled survivor said: "I'd like to dig him up and *kill him again.*"

This condition, what I call the *Immortality Fallacy*, may not be the only reason over half the adults in this country die with no wills and their lives in complete disarray, but I suspect it's the grand prize winner. Maybe another reason unplanned death is so common is that many of the perps are unsophisticated, don't get the legalities behind wills and estates and are just screw-up's who don't have their acts together. Sound like a reasonable assumption?

Suppose there's this guy, a well-connected, Been-Around-the-World kind of guy, but his personal finances are a mess. He's got loans out to a bunch of deadbeats who haven't paid him in years, owns real estate spread out in several states, some of it with no-rent squatters on it and the guy hasn't cashed a paycheck *in months*. He's got a spouse he knows may be profoundly disabled, who can't handle money and his kids are not yet ready to so much as open a bank account. His business has been in shambles for years, he knows better, and yet he hasn't got a will and he's going to die with nobody lined up to manage his jumbled mess of an estate. One more thing: Suppose this guy is *himself* a lawyer, somebody who once drafted wills for clients.

Wow, you'd think this guy must be a helpless putz, somebody who really needs to get his act together. Sounds right, except that what I'm describing comes straight out of the Report of Administration for the Decedent's Estate of Abraham Lincoln, the most revered President of the United States, a man who steered the country through its most deadly war and freed the slaves. The hands-down greatest public figure in United States history died without a will and with a messed-up estate that took years to straighten out. And it wasn't like he was a young man—Lincoln was fifty-six. While it may be no fair picking on an assassination victim for not having a will, Lincoln was, and remains, in good company. Most Americans are in exactly the same boat.

Perhaps it's emotional, superstitious hang ups about going to see a lawyer: When I was a kid, my Italian Grandmother used to carry a bunch of savings account passbooks in a shopping bag she hauled around everywhere. She had discrete, handwritten notes rubber-banded to those passbooks, spelling out who was supposed to get each account at her death. When I asked her why she didn't just go see our neighborhood lawyer and do it right, she'd shake her head emphatically and say, "When you go to the lawyer, *that's* when you're gonna die."

I still hear that a lot. Seems like not much has changed since then. Why is this such a big deal? Because, dead people can't own stuff.

The dead can't legally own property, so every county in every state has a probate court that takes control of dead people's cars and money and houses, and the court hands it all around after you die. When you make no plans and die without a will, the court hands out all that property to a bunch of randomly-selected winners, sort of like the Lottery, although, in fairness, it's a *little* less random. Musical chairs is more like it, where your death is when the music stops. That's our first defined term, *Intestacy,* what happens to your property when you die without a will. It's the state law that probate courts follow when they hand around your stuff to your close or in some cases distant relatives, if you have no will. The opposite, you choosing who-gets-what by signing a will, is called *Testation.*

I'd argue that capitalism and the pursuit of accumulated wealth are almost meaningless, a life-long marathon run on a hamster wheel, if after working, striving and saving for decades you're going to die without a will. Do that, and you let chance, fate and the thoughtless pseudo-will your home state intestacy law has drafted for you, decide what happens to everything you own.

You shouldn't take for granted the ability to give your stuff away at death: For centuries, the European ancestors of many Americans weren't allowed to own anything. That was the privilege of the Crown. People who were willing to kiss Crown fanny and die for the King, were the only ones allowed to own some of the King's property.

Even then, though, *Inheritance*, the right to receive that property at death, was fixed by the King—he got to choose, and by law, he chose only *men*.

Here in America, we weren't much better. It was only about a decade before women got the right to vote that married women were finally "allowed" (by the men) to own property. States enacted so-called "Married Women's Property Acts," so a woman's property no longer simply became property owned by their husbands, when they married. It's only been since the early 1900's that all Americans were first entitled to draw up wills and leave their property to anybody they desired. *Divisibility*, the system where property gets freed up from dead-peoples' hands and passed around at death, became a cornerstone of the legal fabric in America. It would be a stretch to say people fought and died for this right, but it didn't come easy, either.

Now, you get this really important choice about who will some-day own all your stuff after you're gone, but to make that choice, you need to *do something*. And, the choices are virtually unlimited when you make a will. In every state but Louisiana, you can choose to give your property to anybody, and to *Dis-inherit* anybody, the act of over-riding those state intestacy statutes with your own choices. That includes dis-inheriting your kids and even your spouse, although dis-inheriting spouses takes some extra effort in many states, and only works for half of your property in Community Property states, which are primarily most of the West and Southwest.

How can I be so sure folks aren't consciously *choosing* Intestacy, gleefully letting the state pick their beneficiaries? I've drafted over a thousand wills and trusts over the forty-two years I've practiced law, and during that time, *not a single person I've seen has chosen to leave their property to the folks listed in the intestacy statute, in just the way the State does it.* Why is that? Well, for one thing, Intestacy means outright ownership handed out among spouses and kids, and in many States spouses don't get it all, even if the kids are babies—those babies still get handed a check, which, as you can imagine, is a nightmare. If you're not survived by spouses and kids, your stuff gets spread around parents, siblings, nieces and nephews, again in outright fractional shares. No safeguarding the dough from drunks or drug-addled relatives—they just get handed a check, too.

And, if you don't have close relatives, the Intestacy laws go back up your family tree to grandparents and great-grandparents, who are almost always dead, so your property goes back down the family tree and gets sprinkled on folks like second and third cousins twice removed, almost certainly people you've never met and probably nobody you'd choose to get everything you've ever owned. Most people without immediate family would pick friends, an alma mater or favorite charities, but no intestacy statute includes any of those beneficiaries. Intestacy statutes were first dreamed up over a hundred years ago, when America was primarily a giant farm-belt. Those farmers and their cigar-chomping buddies in the law-drafting State Legislatures wanted their land to stay in the family.

To make matters worse, in most states, if you die Intestate and you've got no relatives left on the planet, the local County Board where you lived decides how to spend your dough. I'm sure your neighborhood County Sheriffs' Deputies are swell people, but did you ever figure on working your entire life, just to give them everything you own?

So, if dying *Intestate*, leaving your choices to the state legislature, is such a wrong-headed, bone-headed non-choice of a choice, you'd figure that almost nobody would make such a mistake, right?

Well, no. The percentage of people who do this is staggering. The majority of Americans who die each year, don't do any planning. That's right: Of the almost three million people that die in the U.S. each year, anywhere from *50% to 60%*, in a given year, have no will and have done no post-death planning. That sounds a little abstract, so let's unpack it: Almost 1,600,000 people, on average, die every year in the U.S. without having lifted a finger to decide who gets their stuff. Roughly 80% of them, 1,300,000, lived above the poverty level and have up to or over a million dollars to hand around at death. It's as though the entire population of Dallas Texas, or the combined populations of Seattle and Milwaukee, died each and every year, with enough money to care but no will and no post-death planning. It's like the entire, combined populations of Iceland, the Bahamas and Luxembourg......well, you get the idea.

That many people can't all be wrong for the same reason. Maybe it's not all based on a delusional belief in immortality. Perhaps it's the other well-worn excuse: *It costs too much; lawyers are too expensive; I've worked hard for this money, and I'll be damned if I'm going to spend it on some lawyer.* While you hear that a lot in my business, Howard Hughes, Picasso, Prince and Aretha Franklin all died without valid, lawyer-drafted wills and all of them were zillionaires, so each of them probably could have sprung for the legal fees they would have spent.

Trying to psychoanalyze half the U.S.A. is exhausting, so let me resort to scare tactics. Not convinced it's more important to go see your probate lawyer than whistle past the graveyard? Before I de-mystify this process, and tell you everything a non-lawyer needs to know about it, let me *motivate* you. Here's the first of twenty-three case studies I'll use to try to teach you a lesson. Practicing probate law for over forty years, you see a lot of bad and just plain foolish behavior. While none of these case studies describe my clients, still, I've changed the names, occupations and other identifying details in these scenarios, just to protect the innocent and the not-so-innocent. The bad decisions, non-decisions and screw-ups, however, are real. I'll call this one:

How 'Bout Working Your Whole Life Just to Support the East German Secret Police?

About forty years ago, a young lawyer got appointed by a probate judge to go find a dead guy's missing heirs. Dead guy, we'll call him Schmitz, had no will, but he did have a couple million dollars. He'd never married or had kids, and like a lot of folks in his generation, he'd come over to America in the pre-World War II wave of immigration, so his more distant relatives were still in Europe. He died before the fall of Communist Eastern Europe, so when the lawyer hired an *Heir Chaser,* a private detective who specializes in finding missing relatives, the Chaser had to go fishing behind the so-called Iron Curtain, in what were then the Communist-Bloc countries.

The Heir Chaser followed a trail that led him to a bunch of small country churches in what was then East Germany, looking for birth registries. It turned out that Franz Schmitzenmeyer, the name we'll give the missing heir, was a distant second cousin, twice removed, who was a disgraced member of the East German Secret Police, sitting in a jail cell on the wrong side of the Berlin Wall. Keep in mind, East German Secret Police were generally not nice people, so being a *disgraced* member was a lot like being a too-aggressive linebacker in the NFL—you really had to work at that.

When the lawyer told Schmitz's best friend (who, of course, wasn't getting anything) about the incarcerated hitman who would receive Schmitz's intestate booty, he belly-ached at length about how Schmitz hated Communists and would have wanted his local parish church to get the money, etcetera, etcetera. One more thing: Because they were all still Communists, and with Schmitzenmeyer being disgraced and all, the East Germans ended up confiscating the couple million dollars the lawyer had to deliver to Franz, sitting in his jail cell. But, *hey*, what's so bad about working your whole life, just to support a totalitarian Communist regime that goes against everything you've ever cared about? That's *Intestacy*.

There: Hopefully, I've convinced you that forgoing adequate death planning legal representation and dying without a will are irrational, self-defeating acts.

Now, what *else* are you doing wrong?

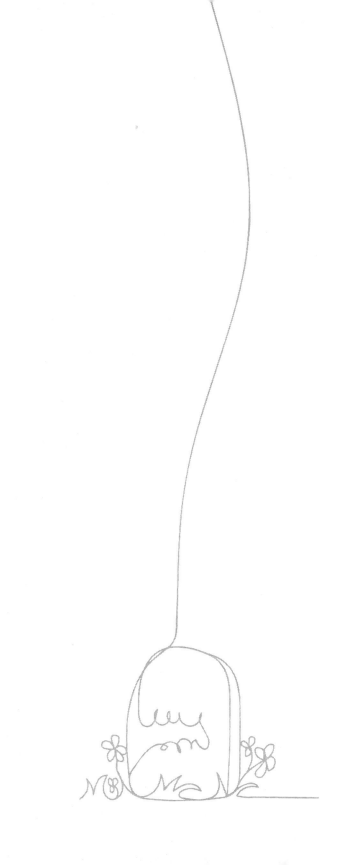

2. JOINT TENANCY: GET ME OUTTA THIS JOINT

Think about this:

Suppose you own a boat—not a yacht, not a big boat, just a boat you scrimped and saved to buy. You like tooling around in it on the weekends, but your kids aren't that into it, so you call around, and eventually you get your buddy Stosh to ride around with you, and one day, while you're driving Stosh around, you die. Now suppose, when your son goes to claim the boat from the cops and retrieve your body, the boat is gone, and so is Stosh. "Where's the boat?" your son asks, and the cops say, "We gave it to Stosh—it's his now," and when your son asks "Why?" the cops say, "Because he was riding around in it when your Father died."

If that sounds weird to you, congratulations: Without an hour of law school, you just figured out what's wrong with *Joint Tenancy*, the form of co-ownership used by just about everybody who simultaneously owns stuff with another person. While Stosh didn't start out as a co-owner of that boat, he essentially inherited it due to a split-second decision by local officials brought about by death of the boat's owner. Joint Tenancy is much like that—a bad thing because it hands out your property at death based on an afterthought (by you), and that result is dictated by strangers (the Legal System where you live). The typical person setting up a joint tenancy gives the process about as much thought as the cops did when they told Stosh to take that boat and vanish.

Joint Tenancy is a kind of death planning self-help that's worse than doing nothing at all. It is so widely used, you'd be justified in thinking my dislike for it makes me a crackpot, so allow me to explain myself. *Joint Tenancy* is when two or more people own something at the same time, *with Right of Survivorship*, which in English means when the first owner dies, his interest is *Extinguished,* and the other owner *Survives*. Sounds harsh, and it is—nothing passes from you to your survivors when you die: You're just treated like you never owned anything in the first place. Doesn't matter if you paid for your house or put the money in that joint bank account from which you are now *extinguished*, you're gone, *poof,* and the survivor owns the house or the bank account, without so much as ever having contributed a dime of the joint property. This is different from other forms of co-owner-ship like *Tenancy in Common*, where your share survives your death and passes under your will.

Joint Tenancy is used primarily to own houses and bank accounts. We'll put aside houses for a moment, since they are usually held between spouses and that's sort of a special case. Let's focus instead on money. Here's where we get to the *afterthought* part. Ever read one of those deposit contracts you sign at the bank when you open an account? Yeah? You're *lying*—nobody reads those things, first, because when you go to the bank, it's a lot like standing in line at the Post Office, second, you're in a hurry, and anyway, *What's the big deal?* You're opening a bank account, not signing up to serve in the infantry in Afghanistan. Besides, the fine print is too small for anybody but an insect to read.

If you even thought about the joint ownership deal with the account, I know what you said: "I want to put my spouse, or my secretary, or my kids, *on the account*....." You figure this will give the second person, your spouse, or your kid, or the secretary who pays your bills, access to the account, sort of a poor-man's power of attorney that you—*phew*—didn't have to pay a lawyer to draft. Here's what you did *not* say: "I want to make a gift at death to this person, and give them the right during my life to withdraw all this money, drain the account and spend it at the casinos." This didn't happen because *nobody's ever said that,* when setting up a joint account.

Since you're not reading the signature-card contract, you don't realize that by creating a joint account, you are giving those other folks you put "on" the account unlimited right during your life to take all the money and run, *without asking or telling you,* even if you're the only one depositing money into the account. And, for sure, you're not reading the part that says the surviving owner gets all the money in the account at your death, however it got there and whoever put it there.

There's a legal cottage industry of post-death litigation over joint accounts. Why? Because once the people who are *supposed* to get your stuff at your death, those folks named in your will, once they find out about these joint accounts and how your money is going to whoever got accidentally "put on" the account, *they want it back.* How's that work? In most states, the laws recognize that nobody reads these signature cards. Those same laws allow your estate beneficiaries to go to court and claim that the joint tenants were just added to the account for *convenience*. No gift at death was *intended*, the joint tenant was just a glorified *agent*, added so he or she could pay bills and make deposits and transfers.

These cases clog probate court dockets around the country, and they're messy, expensive and no joke. A tale of unintended consequences will prove my point.

Blinded by Boring Bank Documents

So, we have a Big Shot Sports Agent, worth oodles of money, and of course, he doesn't sweat the small stuff—his Trusted Secretary pays his bills, juggles his calendar, does his Christmas cards. He sets up a joint checking account and "puts her on it", as he told his spouse, so Trusted Secretary could write checks, make deposits and pay his bills. Big Shot's Trusted Secretary also has access to his payroll and retirement accounts, so she can juggle those too. While Big Shot generally keeps more money in that joint checking account than you or I would, it is usually run down at the end of each month by his mega-bill payments.

That all changes when he gets a bad report from his doctor, a fact he shares with Trusted Secretary, who promptly transfers a million dollars from his other accounts into the "bill-paying" joint account, "Just in case it's needed," she says. When he makes good on the bad medical report and promptly dies, Trusted Secretary shows up at the bank on the way home from the funeral and says, "I want to make a withdrawal—millions, please." The Bankers are suspicious, so they delay the withdrawal and alert the Widow.

The lawsuit brought by his Widow freezes the account, and the case is about *the question*: Did Big Shot intend to make a gift at death to Trusted Secretary (what the signature card/deposit contract *says*), or was Trusted Secretary just added for *convenience*? And, is that million-dollar transfer into the account just before Big Shot's death a little self-help on the part of Trusted Secretary?

These are jury trials, which cost loads and have much more uncertain outcomes than you'd have if you'd just named your Trusted Secretary agent on the account, with signature power (a thing banks offer), which terminates at death and makes no gift of the accounts, but people just *love* joint accounts. So, with your no-lawyer-got-paid-to-set-it-up joint account, what you get is a jury trial at death.

And, how do we know nobody reads the signature cards? Well, in this case, Trusted Secretary's lawyer tried to pull a fast one—he blew up a copy of the three-by-four-inch signature card with the insect-only-readable print, enlarged it to half the size of the average Major League Baseball stadium scoreboard. Then he dragged the giant signature card replica into the courtroom, so the jury could actually read all that gift-at-death fine print. "See," he was arguing, "Big Shot *must* have understood he was making a gift—look at all those big words that say so."

While the Estate's lawyer was convincing the Judge to get the signature card on steroids out of the courtroom, one of the jurors glanced at it.

"So, *that's* what those things say—I've never actually read one before," she blurted out.

After the trial, which tossed out the gift-at-death claim by Trusted Secretary, the Lawyers are polling the jury, and none of them had ever read their bank signature cards, but most of them had joint accounts. And, what did the blurting juror do for a living? That's right, she was *a lawyer*. OK, not a probate lawyer, but, *still*.

Now that we've established that setting up joint accounts often creates an unintended gift at death, you might ask, "Yeah, but who puts a bunch of money in these things? They're easy, no lawyers involved, and it doesn't matter so long as you keep them small?" Well, sure, except your joint tenant can empty the account at any time, and you have no remedy if they do so during your life, so if you don't really intend a gift at death, why not just keep your own money in your own name and do a will for the afterlife? Having somebody raid your bank accounts and then subjecting your heirs to a jury trial at death should be nobody's idea of acceptable collateral damage from saving a few bucks by not doing a will. Yes—many bankers call these things *Will Substitutes*. That's like calling a pair of pliers *a Dentist Substitute*.

Yeah, I know—people like to put their houses in joint tenancy with their spouses, so the house won't need to go through probate at the first spouse's death. What about that? Doesn't sound too scary, does it?

Avoiding probate is actually a bad idea (more about that later), but even if you think it's a not-so-bad idea, there are still drawbacks to having your house in joint tenancy, even with a spouse. For one thing, if your spouse has a gambling problem or they get sued over a bad business deal, your deadbeat spouse's debts can get attached to a jointly-owned house. It's one thing to lose your house because you just can't pay the mortgage, but a whole other tragedy if you lose it just because you wanted to avoid putting it through probate when you died.

If I can't convince you to skip joint tenancy for your house, then, at least, try an alternative: *Tenancy by the Entireties.* Most states provide for this version of joint home ownership, but only for married couples, and while it has the same right of survivorship, no-probate-at-death feature, it doesn't allow your deadbeat spouse to have the house taken by his bookie, loan shark or business partner. Only *joint debts,* I.O.U.'s you *both* sign on for, can get attached to an *Entireties* house. And, if your divorce lawyer forgets to split up your co-ownership of that house after the divorce, *Entireties* property automatically divides upon the divorce—you or your heirs will get your half when you die, no matter what.

The punch line here is that Joint Tenancy is no panacea, and certainly not something that should be used as a death-planning or probate substitute. If you own anything in Joint Tenancy, you're asking for trouble.

3. DON'T DO IT YOURSELF

The doctors and dentists don't have this problem. Nobody goes to their doctor's office, gets a diagnosis like, "You've got a hernia, we need to bring you in for an operation," and replies, "Thanks, doc, but I think I'll just go home and cut it out myself, save a few bucks." Nobody tells the dentist, "I'll drill out my own root canal. I'll be sure to stop before the drill bit hits *my brain*."

Lawyers get this, more often than you'd think. Maybe, like the doctors, we need white lab coats and a secret language full of numbers and un-pronounceable words to scare people off, because without that, folks just assume, "Hey, how hard can it be?" Then, they trundle off, scheming to draft their own wills, take online courses, set up their own bargain-basement perpetual trusts and transfer their houses into joint tenancy, all just to save a few dollars in legal fees. They remind me of the people I see at planning seminars, who say, "I was at the butcher shop the other day, and this guy in line behind me said he set up a corporation and transferred all his stuff into it, and now he gets tax deductions for all his living expenses, food and gas bills, kids' tuition—*everything*—and my butcher said, 'Yeah, I hear that works.'"

True, you can get your hands on all the law books and read them yourself and eventually you'd get the general idea, but when you hire a lawyer, what you're really paying for is collective judgment and experience, as well as professional record keeping. Hiring that lawyer saves you from making the mistakes I'm writing about now.

When I was in College and worked part-time in a gas station as an auto mechanic, we had a sign on the wall in the shop. It read: "Our Rates: $15 an hour; $25 an hour if you *watch*; $50 an hour if you *help*." There's a legitimate point to this warning: Do-it-yourselfers just get in the way. Given a reasonable period of time and practice, almost anybody can do anything, but the probability for error with first-timers never goes away, so that's why you pay somebody who's done it before to cut up your intestines, just to handicap against the possibility of bleeding to death. If you retreat to the attic to draft your own will, I'll venture a guess it will be both the first and last one you draft, without any training, and you wouldn't even want somebody with that track record tuning up your car or cleaning your teeth.

Here's another thing about screwing up that will you draft in your attic: *Once you die, it can't be fixed.* And because you're doing it yourself, you're probably stuffing the finished product in a drawer somewhere, so nobody will see the excellent job you've done until you're six-feet underground, and then all they can do is say, "He did *that*? Guess we'll need to go to Court and pay a bunch of lawyers to sort it out." Of course, that kind of litigation costs bundles more than the $1,000 to $2,000 most lawyers would charge for a basic estate plan and a will, the kind you could try to mimic by candlelight, typing away in your attic.

Think I'm making a big deal out of a harmless case of Amateur Hour?

The Probate Act as Bathroom Reading Material

There's this Old Guy, Bud, a retired bartender who once ran a neighborhood dive bar. His spouse has died. He has no kids, but he's close to his niece and nephew, who've taken care of him and looked in on him for years, as he's lived quietly alone in the house he's owned for decades. He's also accumulated a million bucks, just by working, saving and investing while living like a monk (he's never bought a washer/dryer, instead trudging every week to the laundromat). He's always told Niece and Nephew they get everything when he dies, and shown them his will that says so. He's even told them where he stores the will, so they can find it *if* he dies (I know, makes me crazy, this *if* stuff).

Bud starts to suffer dementia and gets squirrely, so Niece and Nephew take him in to their homes and take care of him until he dies. When they go to find the will, the envelope in his desk that says, "Last Will and Testament" is empty. Soon after that, Nefarious Neighbors show up with a will giving everything to them, drawn up and signed shortly before Niece and Nephew took Bud in to their home. "He was too out of it to do this," Niece and Nephew cry, as they hire a lawyer to fight the bogus new will.

Problem is, their rights are much harder to enforce, and they face a lot of procedural disadvantages in the litigation, because nobody can find that prior will he told them about. Worse yet, Niece and Nephew can't even testify about how that old will gave *them* everything, due to the "Dead Man's Act", a law that blocks testimony from people with a stake in the outcome.

Niece and Nephew turn to Bud's former lawyer, but he has no record of the prior will, because he didn't draft it. "I told Bud he needed to do a will over and over again, but each time I quoted him the fee, he said, 'No thanks'".

Niece and Nephew's lawyer gets a court order so he can go search Bud's house, which, without success in their will contest, will soon belong to Nefarious Neighbors under the new will. After ransacking all the places you'd expect to see valuables, important papers and the like, Lawyer for Niece and Nephew makes his way into Bud's attic. There, Bud has an antique, roll-top desk, complete with reading lamp and comfy chair. When Lawyer rolls back the desktop, he finds a pad of paper, pens, and a dog-eared paperback copy of the State Probate Act, the statutory collection of laws that govern wills, trusts, and probating them after death. He opens the statute book and finds several passages underlined, including sections about how many witnesses you need to make a valid will, what needs to be included in a will, and what needs to be done to probate it at death.

Let's stop here for a moment and take a brief quiz:

Which of the following sorts of people have a good reason to keep a dog-eared copy of the State Probate Act hidden away in their home-office desk:

a. A Probate Lawyer

b. A Probate Judge

c. A Probate Court Clerk

d. An Accountant who does tax work on estates and trusts all the time

e. A Retired Bartender

If you answered "(e)", you might as well throw this book away. I'm obviously not getting my message across to you.

The reason nobody can find evidence of the prior will is that Old Guy Bud drafted it himself, sitting in the attic, paging through the Probate Act as he typed, to make sure he was doing it just right. If he'd hired his attorney to do that will, there'd be copies of it, a record that it was done and what choices he'd made, and, most importantly, a witness (his lawyer) who could testify about the whole thing. That prior story of Bud giving everything to Niece and Nephew, reflected in that prior will, is admissible in evidence in the will contest—it can be enough to convince a jury that Bud meant to give everything to Niece and Nephew, once the doctors describe his dementia. Equally important, a copy of the prior will, now destroyed, could be admitted to probate if Niece and Nephew could prove it was destroyed by Nefarious Neighbors, not by Bud. But Bud, a millionaire attempting to save a thousand bucks, has given Niece and Nephew an uphill battle in a case that should have been an easy win for them.

Niece and Nephew eventually prevail in the litigation, but it costs almost a hundred thousand bucks to prosecute, which ultimately gets charged to the estate, diminishing their inheritance. And, Niece and Nephew are lucky—they're Bud's only intestate heirs. If they'd been just two of a bigger group of heirs, they'd have gone through all this for a much smaller slice of Bud's estate, without that prior will giving them everything. Niece and Nephew want to dig up Bud and ask, "What were you *thinking*?"

Still not convinced about getting advice from somebody with enough experience and judgment to do your will right, and tell you when your choices are dangerous? If those qualities don't get you to a professional for help with your will, how about this: At least, lawyers maintain *files*. And, those files are usually retained forever, either by the lawyer who did the work, or by whoever took over his or her practice when they retired.

And then, there's this: Remember how Picasso, Howard Hughes, Aretha Franklin and Prince, all died without wills? Each of Hughes's and Franklin's estates endured expensive, protracted and melodramatic (some would say *slapstick*) litigation over suspiciously-discovered, handwritten-do-it-yourself, allegedly valid wills. The reason you never hear about such cases occurring when the dead people actually had lawyer-drafted, proper-appearing wills, is because nobody believes that anybody who paid a lawyer to get a professional will, would then go home and say, *"Gee, on second thought, I'll just pull up a chair, sharpen up my pencil and take a crack at writing up one of these wills myself.*" The I-found-this-handwritten-will-stuffed-in-the-couch-cushions types, claiming that the scribbled will they "found" just so happens to leave everything to them, are taking advantage of the vacuum left by lawyer-phobic types who don't have genuine wills.

Sorry about this, but stop complaining and pay the bill……

4. HOW TO AVOID AVOIDING PROBATE

Here's another quiz:

Which one of these is the scariest menace facing U.S. Society today:

a. Internet hacking and cyber terrorism

b. International political instability and the threat of nuclear proliferation

c. Domestic extremists and international terrorists

d. Global warming, plagues and ecological disasters

e. Gun violence and urban street crime

f. Scheming probate lawyers and Judges, conniving to fleece you out of a $250 probate filing fee

If you answered "(f)", boy, have I got a book for *you*.

"How to Avoid Probate," a chunky essay full of forms and do-it-yourself tips, is the mirror opposite of this book. First published in 1965, it's now in something like it's sixtieth printing. It speaks to all the ways you can stand on your head to sidestep the probate process. To me, the book weaves the specter of **PROBATE** as a sinister conspiracy to rob you of your hard-earned money, while enriching a shady, corrupt mini-industry of lawyers, eagerly awaiting an innocent-bunch-of-chumps public.

I suspect that in 1965, one major premise behind the book was exposing a supposed consumer rip-off involving the court process of probating estates. The alleged scheme: The then common (and now *uncommon*) practice of setting attorney fees for handling Probate at a straight percentage of the value of the assets passing through the Probate pipeline. This practice was arguably an unsavory racket because it rewarded lawyers regardless of the particular lawyer's time commitment or the complexity of the representation. The other claim driving this self-help-addled probate phobia was the assertion that the probate process took forever and cost a fortune.

This is now pretty old news. Seven states still *allow* percentage billing (New York, California and Florida are the notables), but the rates are pretty modest (usually, a fraction of one percent, or a point or two) and all states allow you to limit your attorney to an hourly charge by agreement, which is now the norm. In any event, the fees need to be *reasonable,* and the Court gets to decide if you object.

Forty-two years ago, when I started practicing, probate was a pretty clunky process. You needed to hire a court-approved appraiser, who cataloged and appraised *all* of the dead person's stuff—cars, furniture, clothing, *everything*, then you needed a separate appraiser to make a report on the value of your house. All those reports then got filed with the court and mailed to the dead person's creditors, then the local taxing authorities came and rummaged through the dead person's safe deposit boxes. The decedent's bank accounts were frozen until the state-inheritance-tax-collector guys let them go, and yes, the process took a lot of time.

Today, virtually all states have enacted forms of simplified probate, where your lawyer shows up in Court twice: Once to say "Hello" and get your will "admitted", which generally takes five minutes; and once, months (not years) later, to say, "Goodbye, we did our job," which takes about ten minutes. In between, there are no court-appointed appraisers, no requirement for filing inventories or accountings with the court, and if everybody involved agrees or just doesn't care, you usually wait around for a few months and if nobody shows up to complain, you're done. The safe deposit box exams and bank-account freezes are a thing of the past. The average court cost is under three hundred dollars, and lawyer fees are carefully scrutinized by the court. Those fees are now almost universally time-based and competition is fierce. With a straight-forward set of assets and documents (Yes—that means you had a lawyer draft your will and it's not screwed up), the out-of-pocket cost is generally under a thousand dollars, and your legal bill shouldn't be more than a couple thousand bucks, unless you died intestate with complicated heirship or have other problems.

In other words, whatever historical factors drove the attractiveness of probate-avoidance schemes in the Sixties, today probate phobia's a bunch of hooey, albeit still very popular hooey. Some folks would say it's largely responsible for the nasty trends I've been complaining about since page one, and it looks like it's making new converts every day.

Some myth debunking is in order.

Probate really isn't all that complicated or mysterious. First, the court figures out who your intestate heirs are based on an affidavit your lawyer drafts (they get mailed notice). It says pedestrian things that loosely translate to, "Dead Person was married to Sam Smith, and had three kids....and there's nobody else around." Then, you prove up the will by handing it up to the court, where the Judge reviews it to see if it is "self-proving" (most are, if lawyer drafted), which just means it's got magic language about the witnesses and how the will was signed. Then, you don't need to haul the witnesses to the will into court to testify about what happened when it was signed.

Right then and there, once the will is admitted to probate, the court appoints somebody boss, usually an executor named in the will. There are no sureties required, insurance policies on the executor's promise not to rip anybody off, an expense you dodge unless you die intestate or you wrote your will yourself. If you did that, you forgot to say that you don't want sureties—a common mistake by do-it-yourselfers.

Then you go home, wait a while—the time varies state to state—usually three to six months. You publish one of those fine-print squibs in a newspaper nobody reads, telling the world, "Dead guy is dead and if you think he owed you money, come and get It." Typical cost for that publication is a couple hundred bucks. If no claims are filed, you close up shop with that "We did our job" court appearance, and you're done. If that sounds complicated to you, for an experienced lawyer, it's not—most of it is form-driven, and can be handled in a couple of hours of legal work. Yes, you still need a lawyer, just in case something goes wrong or to spot your unusual problems. If it gets complicated, it's because dead people leave their problems behind—unpaid debts, family fights, messed up real estate—not because the process is a scam.

So, where's the conspiracy to rip you off?

If you're a suspicious sort, let me highlight a comparison of the benefits of going through probate versus benefits of *not* going through probate:

Probate Benefits	No Probate Benefits
Absolute, prompt cut-off of creditor claims (hugely important)	No $3,000 in fees and costs
Absolute cut-off of any challenges to the Will	
Cut-off of any challenges to trusts that receive probate assets	
Timely court determination of heirship (also hugely important)	
Ability to cash outstanding checks and collect assets	
Clear record of title, who-owns-what, including property like art and jewelry	
No liability for the executor for distributing property and paying bills	
Beneficiaries free to spend what they get	

Do we see a pattern emerging here?

Yes, it's difficult to go through this process without hiring a lawyer, but most county courts now have programs where you can get a volunteer lawyer appointed if you lack the resources to pay, and if there's little at stake you can even apply to waive the court-filing fee.

Ironically, it's often the people most scared off by the process (and by dramatic stories about what a rip-off it is) that need it the most. A fairly typical situation is people who die with nothing to their name but the house where they lived. Often these folks die intestate, and the house is to be divided between kids or siblings or other intestate heirs. There are often disputes if one heir is living in the house, or if the heirs just need to go through the process of getting the place sold. In those cases, probate is a Godsend, since the heirs can clean up messy fractional ownership of the house and be protected when the place is sold. The Court makes sure everybody gets their share of the proceeds.

There are lots of gimmicky alternatives around, like indemnity agreements, bonds in lieu of probate and summary, one-shot, short-cut court proceedings, all designed to address the irrational fears many people have about the probate process. I've used them all, and the dirty little secret is they are fraught with problems and hidden costs and leave unresolved many of the property headaches and liabilities put to bed by standard probate. This is particularly true with real estate, where probate is often the only way to establish clear title so it can be sold with an unblemished title insurance report. Half the time, people using these short-cuts end up having to go through probate anyway, after the short-cuts fail to clean up everything.

And then, there's the surprise party nobody expects:

The Story of a Man in a Trailer and A Fortune Lost

Back in the Good Old Days, when everybody was reading "How to Avoid Probate," a new lawyer was dealing with a supposedly wealthy dead person. A retired executive—call him Cranch—had died. He had no will, but it didn't appear that he owned much other than a really big house, where he'd apparently poured all his money. The young lawyer, at the insistence of Cranch's two pushy siblings, cleaned up Cranch's estate without probate. This was possible because he'd never married or had kids, and his house and bank accounts were all in—*gasp*—joint tenancy with the two pushy siblings, so it seemed there wouldn't be a need for probate. This was good, siblings argued, because nobody wanted to deal with his complicated heirship—he had a couple of other elderly brothers and a slew of dead brothers and sisters with surviving kids, so he had nieces and nephews scattered all over the place. These were people the lawyer would need to locate if Cranch had any probate property, assets in his name alone, which supposedly he didn't, so pushy joint-tenant siblings gleefully celebrated their good luck in avoiding probate.

Turns out, when pushy brother and sister were cleaning out the house to prepare it for sale, they found a locked vault room in the basement. Inside was a collection of antique, historical photographs, many dating to the 1800's, a set so diverse it included a Lincoln portrait and a large, standing shot of Four Robes, Sitting Bull's second spouse (Like a lot of powerful men, Mr. Bull had several).

"No wonder Cranch didn't have much money," his pushy brother declared, realizing Cranch was spending all his dough on assembling his antique photograph collection.

Pushy brother and sister tried to claim the photos, since the pix were locked away in that joint-tenancy house, but where you store your stuff doesn't determine who owns it. A couple of other heirs fought for the collection, and after a trial the probate court declared the entire collection to be a probate asset in Cranch's intestate estate. As a result, the estate was just getting probated, over two years after Cranch's death. Cranch's heirs were determined as of his date of death nearly two years earlier, which gave rise to a major complication.

While the collection was being sold for millions to a famous museum, young lawyer was dispatched to go meet with Cranch's elderly brother, Elmer, who was supposed to be living like a hermit, without a phone, in a trailer park outside of Jefferson City, Missouri. When lawyer got to the trailer, there was no elderly brother Elmer. Instead, he was greeted by a guy of about thirty, who looked like he could use some inherited dough. He was missing a few teeth and he had a big toe popping out of a hole in his shoe. Lawyer was standing in the doorway of a trailer that was save-the-electricity-dark except for the glow thrown off by a small television, blaringly loud as it barked out a basketball game.

"Elmer's my Grandpa," this guy, Bucky, announced. "He's dead a year now."

When lawyer learned Elmer's date of death was *after* photo-collector Cranch's death, he told grandson that meant his dead grandpa Elmer was an heir of now-mega-sized Cranch's estate. His dead grandpa Elmer had inherited a million dollars, and Bucky was going to need to re-open grandpa Elmer's estate, so they could collect Elmer's share of Uncle Cranch's photo-collection booty.

"Grandpa didn't have no estate—all he had was this trailer, which went to my Daddy, and then to me, when my Daddy died, last year. None of 'em had wills."

You guessed it: Neither the estates of Elmer or his son—Bucky's father—went through probate. Their share of their rich uncle Cranch's *probate estate,* was in turn a probate asset for both of them, ultimately destined to pass to grand-nephew Bucky, if he was indeed Elmer's grandson. Problem was, Bucky's heritage was a little hard to nail down—he admitted he was born out-of-wedlock, and while out-of-wedlock children could claim their father' intestate estates, the problems with proof were complicated, particularly without biological evidence like DNA, which, at that time, wasn't yet standard equipment for heirship cases.

Poor Bucky got locked into an heirship fight with his father's siblings, who would prevail against him if he couldn't prove "By clear and convincing evidence" that he was his father's child. Unfortunately, his now-dead father never acknowledged Bucky's paternity in writing, and his father was no longer around to testify. Every break went against Bucky the maybe-grandchild—Dad had been cremated, so no blood tests were possible, and his father always fought paying child support, claiming "Not my kid," so the paper trail was bad. In the end, this newfound heir of an heir of an heir would not be able to prove his heirship to grandpa Elmer, now that his own father was dead.

There'd been no probate and no determination of heirship when both his father and grandfather died. Bucky lost out to father's siblings.

If everybody who could have probated anything had done so timely, Bucky would have received everything. Now, even title to the trailer with the honking television, *even the television,* was up for grabs.

Ultimately, Bucky missed out on the million and the trailer, which he otherwise would have successfully inherited, if all these estates had been probated promptly when the succession of dead people each passed away.

But, I'm sure Bucky could at least take comfort in knowing that he and all his ancestors got to *Avoid Probate,* for a while, anyway.

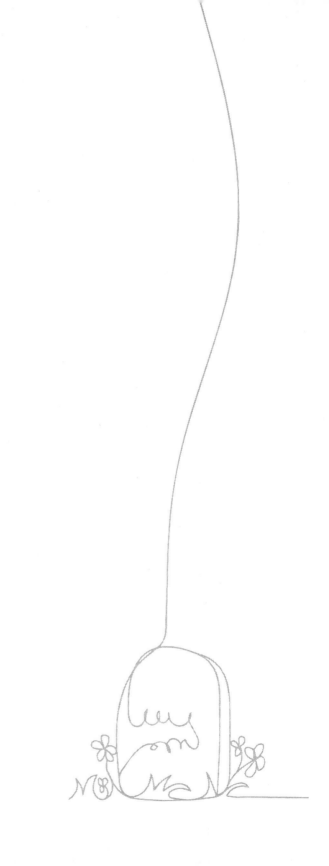

5. WILLS: THE EXECUTION CONFERENCE IS NOT A SEMINAR ON THE DEATH PENALTY

When you get right down to it, there isn't much to a will.

It needs to be in writing, signed by the *Testator* (that's you), and witnessed by at least two disinterested people (folks who don't get anything under the will). The witnesses need to see you sign it and then sign it in your presence, at your invitation or direction.

You can write it on anything: There's a famous case where a farmer wrote his will on the side of a live cow, which obviously complicates submitting that will to the probate court, but yes, that's still a valid will. You can write it *with* anything: A recent case involves a wise-guy testator who wrote the will in blood, and no, it doesn't need to be *your* blood, just in case you have somebody else's blood handy. It doesn't need to be typed or even bound or stapled, although without page numbers an unbound will causes problems, but again, if the Court can sort it out, it's still a valid will.

Technically, there doesn't need to be much of *you*, either, to make a will. You need more mental skills and abilities to buy a used car than you need to be able to validly make your will. The standard loosely translates to, "Hey, you O.K. in there? Got any idea who these people are that you're naming in that will?" Referred to generally as "Knowing the natural objects of your bounty and the testamentary nature of the transaction," you probably need to have more of your marbles to choose the *color* of that used car. There's a reason this capacity standard is so low: Most people are old when they sign their wills, so if you set the mental with-it standard too high, too many people would flunk.

Right about now, you're thinking, If this is one of the most important moves of your life, shouldn't you need to be more glued together to pull it off?

Well, no.

These testation decisions are pretty basic stuff:

- Do I want to avoid taxes where possible? (Yes, always).
- Do I want my spouse, otherwise my kids, to get my personal assets like cars and furnishings? (Almost always, yes).
- Do I want to hold up property in trust if the kids are young? (Usually).
- Do I want to split the booty between my favorite charities or my family and my spouse's family if nobody else is around? (Most times).

People with more complicated plans and more valuable stuff usually use trusts, and in most states, if the trust can be changed until your death, the same loosey-goosey mental capacity standards apply to signing one of those.

The key is that, with a lawyer involved, the courts will assume you communicated with the attorney and the stuff you wanted is in the will. Nobody is fooling anybody about the technical provisions in the fine print: Just like those nasty joint-tenancy signature cards, nobody thinks you actually read, much less understood, that part of the document. The courts who need to enforce wills are just willing to figure you blessed those provisions during the back and forth between you and your attorney. That's the reason many states have rules prohibiting anybody but a lawyer from drafting wills and trusts—because the courts understand there's complex material in there that only a lawyer should explain to you and decide whether or not to include or exclude—not because it's a nasty conspiracy to make you spend money on lawyers.

So, the process of setting up and executing your will isn't too complicated, it's really not that expensive, hopefully by now I've convinced you to go to a lawyer and do it, so what could possibly go wrong?

Turns out, lots, and it's often the silliest of screw-ups.

There's a reason your lawyer's office has no drive-thru: These things take time, usually two or three meetings between you and your lawyer, and then some lawyer-thinking and drafting time. After these on-the-clock get-togethers with your lawyer, like most folks, you're thinking, "How much is this costing me?" And inevitably, when the lawyer finishes your will and maybe your trust, you say, "Hey, just send it out here and I'll sign it up at home."

Bad idea. Remember the stuff about witnesses? It's easier to screw up than you'd think. You and the witnesses need to sign in plain sight of each other, and that means same room, same time, same "line of sight". Lawyers call it "An Execution Conference," and no, that's not an international summit on the death penalty; it's your lawyer supervising the signing of the documents with you in his or her office. That way, you don't get any of the following, all of which I've seen, sometimes more than once:

- "I brought it to the laundromat after I signed it and got a couple guys there to sign....."

- "He was in bed in the other room, scribbling on the will in there, and he yelled at me to come get it and go get somebody to sign as a witness...."

- "We got a couple of folks in the E.R. to sign while we were waiting, but then one of the guys died...."

- "I just had my kids sign it for me....."

- "Don't know who they were. We were at the bank and we grabbed a couple that were waiting in line and forgot to ask them where they live...."

All of these creative approaches threaten the validity of the will—You can't have beneficiaries like your kids sign, you can't break up the signing ceremony so the signatures aren't simultaneous, and if you can't find the witnesses at the time of probate, it could be a problem, particularly if there's a will contest.

I've seen more wills upended by mishandled execution, just to save a few bucks by not going to the lawyer's office to sign. And I once had a retired probate judge tell me the only witness she cared about in a will contest was the drafting lawyer, who then, "....Put the will in front of the testator, his client, explained it one last time, and made sure the guy was OK when he signed...." Can't have that if you do it yourself at the laundromat.

And then, there's this:

The True Story of the Will and the Exploding Cookie Jar

Nobody expects their cookie jar to explode like a hand grenade, but that's not a good reason to store your will in there. The same is true of your underwear drawer, the space between the Corn-flakes and Wheaties on your kitchen shelf or that secret space under the closet floor where you hide a wad of currency and a roll of quarters, anticipating the apocalypse.

Take the case of Lula, who lived quietly in a two-flat while renting out the two-flat next door, both properties that had been in her family for eighty years. The neighborhood had been old and kind of worn down, so at first the places weren't worth much. But then, the neighborhood began to improve, and suddenly, Lula was a millionaire.

Lula had the sense to go to a lawyer and do a will, one that really mattered because she was dividing stuff unevenly between her kids, holding the share for her wayward daughter in trust.

When Lula asked the lawyer where she should store the will, the lawyer inquired about any safe places in her two-flat. After determining Lula lacked the usual suspects—file cabinets, portable safes and strong boxes, the lawyer, with all the brain-power and judgment that comes with two graduate degrees, told Lula, "Some folks keep their wills in the meat drawer in the fridge—it's fire-proof and will even survive a nuclear explosion," that latter part being an urban myth that lacks substantiation.

The meat drawer is where the will sat for a few years, until Lula's daughter Wanda asked about the will's whereabouts. Wanda was understandably skeptical about the soundness of the meat-tray advice, so she asked her own lawyer, who said, "Don't keep it in the fridge—what if stuff spoils in there? I tell my clients to keep their wills in the cookie jar. You'll always be able to find it there."

By now, you may be wondering why this orgy of bad advice became notorious, and the answer is that a year later, the two flat burned to the ground in a fire that obliterated the cookie jar, Lula and the will. Her lawyer was sorting through the mess, filing insurance claims and trying to get a copy of the carbonized will admitted to probate, and no, the moral of this story, as one of the heirs once pointed out, is *not* that the will probably would have survived in the fridge.

The point is, people, *get a safe deposit box at your local bank and put the will in there*. Almost every bank has one, and the typical annual rent is forty-five dollars, about what you pay for four beers at your average major-league baseball game. No fridge, no sock drawer, no underwear drawer, and I can't tell you how many fire-singed, burned-archeological-dig-looking document fragments I've pulled out of those supposedly fire-proof, home-safe, metal boxes. Use a major bank, so they don't terminate your box lease, and don't put valuable property in there—just documents like your will.

And, tell your lawyer which bank you picked and what box number they gave you. The crack I made about the space between the Wheaties and the Cornflakes comes straight out of a year's-long fight over a missing will. The will eventually turned up when they cleaned out the dead guy's apartment and his kids found it, safely tucked between those cereal boxes, since dead guy apparently liked to take the will down and review it during casual breakfasts. If this is you, you need both a hobby *and* a safe deposit box, but if I still haven't convinced you, at least tell your lawyer which cereal selection is your favorite.

6. "X" MARKS THE SPOT: PERSONAL TREASURE MAPS AND GUIDES TO YOUR STUFF

Know what's the hardest thing in the world to get rid of? It's not a case of the shingles or your drunken college roommates; it's *a boat*. Not a yacht or even a fancy, antique wooden boat, but the kind of boat most boat people have—that twelve-foot fiberglass sailboat or that fourteen-foot outboard, the kind with those clanking, red gas cans that are also impossible to dispose of once you don't need them anymore. The people who want these kinds of boats already have them, and boats cost money to store unless you live on a farm and have space in your barn. So, dying with one of these vessels is pain in the neck for your executor, who's supposed to turn that boat into money. The thing is, most boat people have *a boat guy*, somebody who services boats, stores them for a living, and just plain knows boat-world, somebody who could be invaluable unloading a small boat nobody wants. But nobody knows about *your* boat guy, unless you leave a note for people, with his name, and address, and, most importantly, *his phone number*.

What about *guns*? You shouldn't be surprised to learn that with more guns than people out in circulation, dead gun owners tend to have more than just one. And, it also shouldn't be shocking to learn that guns, too, are hard to get rid of, because there are *rules.* You can't just hand them out to anybody you want. In some states, you can't even ship them to folks, since your executor is not a registered gun dealer. There's a good chance, though, that unless your gun owner was a crackpot, he or she has a reliable gun dealer, a *gun guy*, if you will, who can help.

What do these things have in common? Only that, with some guidance provided by you in the form of *instructions*, your family's job of finding and disposing of your stuff gets a lot easier. There ought to be a federal law that requires you to sit down at age sixty and draw up a Guide To Your Stuff, starting with a written inventory of your tangible property, important facts about it, as well as a list of who has what, who knows what, and where to find things.

What should be included? Let's start with instructions about that tangible property, items like furniture, art, vehicles, jewelry and the like—the things that often have sentimental value that outweighs their monetary value. In America, people tend to have *a lot* of this stuff, and it is the bane of every probate lawyer's existence. If I had my way, every will would begin with, "At my death, *burn my tangibles,"* but people love their stuff, so that's not going to be popular advice. Still, you really don't want a laundry list in your will of knick-knacks and Jim-cracks in the form of formal bequests of specific items to friends and relatives, even though you may have very specific wishes about who gets what.

Any will that contains a bunch of clauses like, "My authentic, designer, red and white polka dot earmuffs to my cousin Phyllis, who always complimented me when I wore them," should subject the person who signed it to a hefty fine, since imprisonment is no longer an option. It badly complicates probate, as each recipient of this stuff has to get formal notice when you first go to court, and then sign a receipt when you close. Should those silly earmuffs be missing when your executor is rummaging through your closet looking for them, there's going to be a special court mini-trial over those earmuffs: Are they missing? Did dead person throw them away before she died? Did an appraiser or one of dead person's kids steal them?

The best way to make a meaningful disposition of your tangible property is to start your instruction memo with an inventory of your important or valuable tangibles, along with a list of any specific gifts you want to make, and equally important, where to find the stuff and where to locate the people you want to get it. Your lawyer can put a provision in your will that tells your executor to honor this list, without making the entire list a part of the actual will document, thus keeping it out of the lawyer's and the Court's hair. It also keeps it out of the Public Eye, if you're concerned about privacy, which you should be if the list includes your erotica collection or antique torture devices.

True, this exercise requires you to actually take stock in and locate all your tangible property, which in my experience nobody living wants to do. But, if you don't do it and your instruction document or, God forbid, your will actually contains a lot of specific bequests of stuff, then your lawyer and an appraiser will need to hunt it down after you're gone. And, they charge by the hour for this sort of work, both as fair compensation and as a means of punishing you for this sort of silliness.

While we're on the subject of will provisions dealing with your tangible property—furniture and furnishings, jewelry, vehicles, etcetera—one thing to never, ever put in your will, like there should be a federal death penalty for anybody who does this (relax, you're dead anyway), is a provision that says, "Divide my tangibles *equally* among my children *as they decide*." This will *never* happen, requires convoluted joint effort between an appraiser and a referee whistling fouls against your squabbling heirs, all spooling out in a mix of emotion and greed. Instead, let your executor decide how to divvy up the remaining things, once you've laid out in your instruction memo the specific gifts you want to make. And, whatever you do, *don't* tie the division among your kids to the goal of equalizing the value of the stuff that everybody receives. Nobody ever agrees on who gets what and values, plus it's a logistical nightmare. The last time I experienced an "equal value as the kids decide" clause, the lawyers needed to rent an abandoned airport hangar, pile up and tag all the dead woman's stuff, then give the kids shopping carts and have them run around grabbing items, with a timer ticking away in the background.

Next comes the seemingly boring part that is actually quite important: The guide to who everybody is, what everything is, and where to find it and them. Assume that whoever is reading your memo is clueless about your financial life, so that person (your spouse or your kid or your friend or a bank), acting as your executor, needs to be pointed in the right direction. Identify your lawyer, with contact information. If this instruction memo is not in your safe deposit box, shame on you, but then be sure to identify your safe deposit box, by bank location and box number, and describe where you keep the box key—something your lawyer should know anyway. If you have an insurance agent, identify her with a list of policies, by number and insurer, and indicate the location of the original polices (which should also be your safe deposit box, but, if not, say where you parked them). List who to contact at your employer: Typically, you'll have bene-fits there that need to be collected and handed out to beneficiaries. Finally, list your financial assets—bank accounts, brokerage accounts, any place you parked money or securities, and list account numbers, locales, and passwords, if necessary. Keep this document safe, given this sensitive information.

Deal with online information—not just access to online banking sites, but also your email and social media accounts, where you may be getting invoices and have other valuable financial information. If you look into the official way to do this, your head will explode. There's all kinds of laws, like the "Fiduciary Access to Digital Assets Act", and elaborate instructions the online companies post, with clunky advice like, "Be certain to establish Digital Shrines and a Legacy Contact, consistent with your computer's stored cyber intelligence and resort to Password Reset settings....." I'm sixty-six, and to me, that sentence reads, "Blah blah, blah blah blah your computer's blah blah, blah blah blah...."

There's a much less formal way to beat these online providers at making you contort yourself into a cyber-pretzel to satisfy their commercial stranglehold on your data: Give user names and passwords for online banking, bill paying, email and social media accounts in your instruction sheet. Yes, the service providers will argue you're violating the user agreements for those online and social media services. But there's a legal response to that, too.

If you're worried about offending the Service Agreement Gods, then make sure you go through formal probate (You knew that was coming), and give this information to your executor. While the social media companies have fought for years informal, post-death account access by your family members (as in, without *their* consent), they are losing, and in most states if the new user is your executor, he or she is legally protected for essentially hacking your accounts.

In the same vein, give access passwords to your personal computers in the memo. And, be sure if you use fingerprint or facial recognition login security on your computer, you take advantage of the alternate log-in options offered, and include that information in your memo. While that stuff gets marketed as a personal security device to protect you when those burglars with time on their hands break into your home and sit around at your computer, trying to guess your passwords, (*Right*....), it's really designed to defeat the kinds of informal, shared access to your computer I'm suggesting you provide with your instruction memo—good for the tech companies, bad for you.

Do the same thing with your smartphone, and update the memo when passwords change.

This instruction memo contains a lot of information that can be dangerous in the wrong hands, so if you're not keeping it in your safe deposit box, best to give it to your probate lawyer, who can store it securely for you.

If you've got a collection—valuable stuff like art or antique dictionaries or famous autographs—get it insured, and make sure a copy of the policy is with the instructions memo. It will help identify what's in and out of the collection, important if you specifically give it to somebody in your will. Yes, valuable collections *should* be specifically, expressly given away in your will, unlike the claptrap sitting around your house that isn't worth the cost of hauling it away, even if it stares at you from the kitchen counter every morning. How do you tell the difference? If the stuff's uninsurable, you probably shouldn't be collecting it. Baseball scorecards, scented candles and used birdfeeders are all collections I've seen disposed of post-death. Trust me, the Smithsonian doesn't want anything that can't be insured for millions.

What made me a convert on these Instruction Memos?

Three Hundred Fifty-Two Wallets, Including One in the Toilet Tank

An elderly couple of siblings, Karl and Lottie, holed up much of their lives in a shared apartment. Karl was pretty Old World and not very enlightened. He kept the finances, did the taxes, paid the bills, and left the cooking and cleaning up to Lottie (I know—you're thinking, "Too bad he's dead—what a *catch*.")

Anyway, Karl dies first, and in trying to get their things in order for probate, taxes and the like, their lawyer asks, "Where *is* everything?" Lottie kind of glances around the place, waives a dismissive hand in the air, and says, "I don't know—*Karl* took care of everything." "OK," the lawyer asks, "did he keep any records, copies of anything, names, phone numbers, stuff like that?" "Yeah," Lottie replies, "I think, mostly in his wallets."

Note the use of the plural, *wallets*, there.

"He had more than one?" the lawyer asks. Youbetcha, he did. Turns out Karl had a *thing* about wallets. Lottie figures he bought a new one just about every month, and as she's explaining the least erotic leather obsession in America, the lawyer starts opening drawers. Wallets are literally piled in drawers, storage bins, a wire-mesh trash can in the walk-in closet, *everywhere.* The medicine chest, the cabinet under the kitchen sink, hat boxes in the closet, every place you can put a wallet, there's wallets.

Ever lift that porcelain lid on the toilet tank? Well, in this case, the lawyer did, and sure enough, there was a wallet in a plastic baggie, strapped to the inside of the lid.

The lawyer inventories them and stops counting at three hundred fifty-two, thirteen short of one for every day of the year. And, Lottie is right about Karl's file system—as the lawyer starts fishing through each and every wallet, there are hand-written notes creased into the money sleeves and carefully multi-folded into the clear plastic card holders of each wallet. There's no rhyme or reason, no organization, just every transaction Karl's ever undertaken, crammed into some tiny space in one of those wallets.

It takes *months* for an army of paralegals and lawyers to sort the whole thing out, and half the time, the notes just tell you there's more stuff out there: "See list of donations to the Church on note in tan wallet" (There are *dozens* of tan wallets). After it's as sorted out as it's going to get, their financial life is probably half as deciphered as it ought to be, and the only logical conclusion to be drawn is that Karl was an eccentric pack rat who wanted to torture his probate lawyer.

"I told him to make some kind of list," Lottie says, "But all he said was, 'People lose lists—but nobody loses their *wallet.*'"

Finally, a word about Pets: You wouldn't trust the care of your kids to your probate lawyer and you shouldn't trust your pets to the lawyers, either. While many states let you actually bequeath pets in your will, that's not a good idea—your executor then needs to inventory Fido and Fluffy like they're a car or a bank account, get a receipt when she hands them off to "the beneficiary", and report to the court generally about their whereabouts.

If you have a pet and are over fifty, line up a friend ahead of time and arrange for them to take your pet if something happens to you. Make sure to give detailed information about this arrangement in your Instruction Memo. Shortstop the Dog and Paprika the Cat should not themselves be given any money, even though a lot of states now have statutory provisions for setting up trusts for pets, a dumb idea whose time has apparently come. Never require that they be "put down" and stuffed. That would be illegal in most states if your executor carried it out. You can provide a cash bequest for your designated animal caregiver in your will if money is an issue. Pet custody is better dealt with by prior arrangement, not by court order.

7. AINT LOVE GRAND? PRE-MARITAL AND POST-MARITAL AGREEMENTS

I'll admit that if I'd asked my spouse-to-be for an agreement that would limit my obligation to pay her off if we got divorced, she would have told me to stuff it, and I would have remained unmarried, my bicycle and my garage-sale furniture safely protected from the ravages of a potential marital split. So, when I say that most folks, before tying the knot, ought to at least *consider* a so-called *Premarital Agreement, Pre-nuptial,* or *Pre-Nup*, as they're often called, it may sound a little hypocritical. Don't let that stop you from getting one.

Pre-Nuptial Agreements, legal documents you sign before you walk down the aisle, spell out who gets what and mostly who *doesn't* get what, in property division between spouses in the event of death or divorce. These used to be considered sort of creepy and therefore unenforceable in most states. That's all changed, and they're now recognized in most states, thanks in large part in reaction to the realities of the laugh-fest that is modern-day divorce.

The first time I walked into a divorce courtroom, this is what I heard:

Lawyer 1, (shouting): First he slept with his *doctor*, then he slept with his *nurse*, then he slept with his *dentist*, then, you guessed it, he slept with his dental hygienist—I mean, the AMA and the ADA spend less time rooting around in the medical profession—

Lawyer 2, (interrupting): He's doing it *again*. Every time we come in here, it's *delay, delay, delay*—

Lawyer 1, (also interrupting): We just want to stop him from draining the accounts and spending it all on trolling Rush Street for his next underage girlfriend.

Lawyer 2, (pointing at his opponent): The only thing anybody's trolling for around here is his *fees,* filing these pointless motions, and while we're at it, you should tell his client to wait until the separation order's entered to start hitting on her personal trainer.

Judge: Can we just stick to the issue, which if I remember correctly is—

Lawyer 1, (again interrupting, this time interrupting *the Judge*): His client ripping off—

Lawyer 2, (interrupting): No, it's how many times we need to come in here, just to put the screws to his lying, greedy reptile of a client.

Judge: Look, I've got a crowded docket this morning, so if you can't agree on when to set the next status date, I'm going to have my clerk just assign one.

That's right: All that "...You're a so-and-so and I *hate* you...." stuff is because they are arguing about the next *status date*, a nothing hearing where nothing happens, where the Court just checks in with the lawyers to see if the parties are making any progress on pre-trial business.

The reason I'm sharing this joyful little exchange is to show that the real reason to consider a prenuptial agreement is not, as people assume, because it makes your pay-out in the divorce smaller (that *might* happen); it's to prevent fighting over *everything*. If you go into the divorce process already knowing who gets what, it tends to diffuse the intense, my-financial-life-is-on-the-line bickering that breeds all that nearly senseless fighting over the small stuff—like whether the next time the lawyers go to court is a Tuesday or a Wednesday. Endless fighting isn't just juvenile and annoying: it costs money, takes time and creates risks of uncertain outcomes.

Unlike the moralistic Fifties, when I was born, divorce today is not about who caused the marital breakdown by cheating, abusing or doing other bad stuff. That used to drive divorce cases, because you needed to show the other spouse was *at fault,* meaning they were sleeping around and you weren't. Eventually, people came to think it was sort of barbaric to only let folks who hated each other get out of a marriage when one of them was completely innocent of marital wrongdoing. By 2010, all fifty states had *No-Fault Divorce,* which could be unilaterally kick-started by either spouse, just because they could no longer endure looking at each other in the bathroom mirror in the morning.

With no-fault divorce the norm, even without a pre-nup, the fighting is now all about "Who gets what and how much you gonna pay?" Most states have a form of equitable property division, which means everything that got earned or bought or saved during the marriage can be carved up and given in chunks to either spouse, based on everything you can think of, everything *except* who's a bigger dirt-bag. Who cheated on who, who's the drunk, who ran out on who doesn't matter anymore—divorcing parties argue about that fault stuff *just to argue*—no matter that it no longer impacts property split-up or maintenance (what used to be called *alimony*) and child support.

What matters for the property division is who makes more money at their job, who has greater future earning capacity, who squirreled away the most money, who's going to have the bigger slice of custody time raising the kids, and yes, sometimes, who stands to inherit more. This last factor is relevant not because inheritances will get divided between the spouses in the divorce—inheritances will just impact how sympathetic the court is to the richer spouse when cutting up the property pie, the law in all but four states. Once those issues are shaken up in the equitable division bag, a legal knife cuts through the property, and then the court rules on which spouse will owe the other spouse monthly support, and how much.

Even without these Pre-Nuptial agreements, inherited property doesn't actually get carved up or divided between spouses: In most states, it's treated as *Separate Property*, meaning it stays with whoever brought it to the marriage, whether you already got it before the marriage or stand to inherit it in the future. True, it can be difficult to sort out what's Separate Property and what's not, but if you keep it in separate accounts, it doesn't get mixed in with Marital Property, the stuff that gets handed out to winners and losers in a divorce.

And, child support can't be set in a Pre-Nup, because it can't be set by agreement—the Courts always reserve the right to determine how much the kids will cost each month, based on the needs, lifestyles and the best interests of the kids.

You should be asking, right about now: If I'm careful keeping my stuff separate so I don't need a Pre-Nup to protect family-inherited money from the other spouse, and I can still get zapped with whatever the Court thinks is the monthly cost of raising my kids, what good is a Premarital Agreement?

Remember those folks screaming about how much they hate each other, *in front of a judge*, all of it over when's the next time they come into Court to do nothing? Well, everything in divorce is like that, and it tends to infect the lawyers as well as the warring spouses. What a Pre-Nuptial Agreement buys you is freedom from that scene, so all that's left for the Court and those grizzled divorce lawyers to haggle about is child support. And, in most states, there are *guide-*

lines about child support, based on what your paycheck W-2 looks like, essentially setting the payout at a percentage of that W-2 take-home pay, considering how many kids you have and who has to care for them more often.

Things you can agree in a Pre-Nup *not* to fight over:

- Whether either spouse will have to pay to support the other—Complete cross waivers of spousal support, "I don't pay you and you don't pay me," are enforceable;

- Decisions about who gets how many of the "Elvis Shopped Here" Mini Mart franchises the couple accumulated during the marriage;

- Who gets to keep the house, the motorcycle and the spices off the spice rack;

- Whether either spouse has to give the other money from their pension or maintain life insurance; and

- Who pays the lawyer's bills for the divorce—without this, one spouse can end up paying both.

"Who cares about the stupid spice rack?" you may ask. I've seen divorces so contentious that the court needed to enter an order dividing up the spice rack: "Husband gets oregano, Wife gets chili pepper....." Why would anybody *care* about who gets what off the spice rack? They *don't*—they just hate, hate, hate each other, having suffered the greatest betrayal known to mankind, so they fight about *everything*.

And, that's where the Pre-Nuptial Agreement comes in. Why not try to decide what happens *before* you get married, while there's all that bliss going on, instead of when you're breaking up, and the only thing to keep you from killing each other is fear of incarceration? In theory, you'll both make more rational decisions, and since you both need to have lawyers (the agreements are unenforceable unless both sides hire attorneys), you won't do anything foolish. You're thinking, "Won't this take some of the *bliss* out of the process?" Yeah, that is a drawback, and it's one reason most states' lawyers' ethics opinions prohibit a lawyer handling Pre-Nup negotiations from telling you, "If I were you, I wouldn't marry this jerk." We're not qualified to give that advice, even though it has crossed my mind *a lot* in these cases, particularly when I'm representing the poorer spouse.

If inherited property is protected even without Pre-Nups, then why should people who have inherited property, or expect to get it someday, sweat getting Pre-Nup's? Because, the court can still consider inheritances when it decides how many of those marital-property mini-mart's you're going to keep or give away. *How much future inheritance should count in the split-up-of-other-stuff sweepstakes, is one of those things people fight about endlessly, because you don't know when you're going to inherit, or how many distributions you'll actually receive from that trust Grandma set up. If you're the spouse that's someday is going to inherit, it seems unfair to have that count against you when it's all just a future, *potential* bonanza. Still, the court is likely to consider it *now*—unless, of course, marital property division is already set with a Pre-Nup. Then, it's out of the court's hands.

The other advantage of having a Pre-Nup to protect future inheritance is it curbs the involvement of your elders, who love poking their noses into your divorce. I've never seen a parent or grandparent that didn't have intense, emotional opinions about the extent family money should enter into this process, as in, "Over *my dead body* will someday-to-be-divorced spouse get a *dime* of Goldmine family money," being a typical, measured response.

All of this can be settled before you walk down the aisle. You just need two fiancés, two lawyers and complete financial disclosure of what everybody brings to the table. Then, once you've signed a Pre-Nup, all you need to fight over in the divorce is child support, so it's a pretty snappy divorce proceeding. The Pre-Nup will almost always be enforced, unless it is *unconscionable*, meaning, like, the zillionaire spouse keeps everything, and the poor spouse just gets the wooden bowl and spoon he brought to the marriage—so lopsided it shocks the Court's conscience. So, give each other *something* under the Pre-Nup, and it's likely you are done.

And, if you miss the boat, many states allow for the execution and enforcement of Post-Marital, or Post-Nup, agreements, signed after the marriage date. While similar in structure and purpose to Pre-Nups, Post-Nups have one important difference: Since you're already married, nobody's in a big hurry to sign, and often they just don't get done. Yes, that means there's an element of coercion in the build up to and negotiation of Pre-Nups, which is the reason each spouse *must* have a lawyer for the document to be valid and enforceable.

On the positive side, with a Post-Nup you can do something impossible with Pre-Nups: Accomplish a waiver of certain retirement accounts, like Pensions and Profit-Sharing Plans. The 1984 Retirement Equity Act, or "REA", requires that all such plans pay to a surviving spouse when a married employee dies. That right can only be waived by *a spouse*, with a notarized waiver, so a Pre-Nup won't cut it, since you're not yet spouses when you sign a Pre-Nup; almost-spouses don't count. Whether you want your spouse to waive so you can designate your secret girlfriend as beneficiary of your pension plan, or you just have legitimate tax-planning objectives (see Chapter 19), you need to obtain this waiver with a Post-Nup, or with an amendment to your Pre-Nup which is signed after the marriage takes place.

So, getting one of these Pre-Nups in place locks in your rights in event of divorce, and, even better: You get to pay your estate planning lawyer, generally a good-mannered, part-time little-league-coach sort of person, just a few bucks to negotiate and draft this thing. Then, if you get divorced, you pay that snarling divorce lawyer almost nothing.

Not Convinced?

Who Needs One of Those Pre-Nups, Anyway?

Maxine, a young accountant, has some bonus money that's just come her way. A trust set up by an elderly Aunt has also terminated, and she's collected almost a hundred thousand bucks, which is still lying around in her checking account, while she decides where to park it.

She's about to get married to a guy ten years older, who has two kids from his prior marriage.

"You really should think about doing a Pre-Nup," her lawyer advises. "He's got support obligations to those kids, and you've been taking off in your career, and then there's the inherited dough—wouldn't it be a good idea to keep it all separate?"

"I don't know," she hesitates. "Brad would hate it—he thinks it shows a lack of commitment and it's a bad omen (Brad is into *Omens*) if we start hoarding and separating money now, so early in the marriage."

Divorce lawyers *love* somebody like this—they call them *Prospective Clients.*

So, no Pre-Nup, they get married and one night, after dinner and a movie, Maxine and Brad are walking back to their apartment. They pass a used dress shop, sort of a women's antique clothing boutique, where the apparel is organized in sections by the decade of its design. The thing is, it's a Saturday night and the place is *packed*, crawling with customers, some browsing, some buying and everybody just having a good time pawing through the off-beat get-ups.

They wander in. After a while they strike up a conversation with the owners, a couple of out-of-it hippies living in some kind of time warp and it's obvious they're just doing this because they love it. As the hippie couple shows Maxine and Brad around, the evening winds down, it's close to midnight and as the last customers leave, Maxine whispers to Brad, "I think this place has a lot of potential."

Hmmmm, Brad is thinking. He whispers, "These two sensitive-eyed vegetarians have no idea what they're sitting on. Why don't we offer to buy the place—everything, the store, the name, the exclusive right to franchise it? You run back to the apartment and get your checkbook, and I'll see if I can wrangle the place out of them before they realize what's happening."

Maxine retrieves her checkbook, the one for her account which still contains almost hundred thousand plus bucks of her money—*inherited money*—while Brad starts negotiating. Soon they're coming to terms and the price has escalated to the entire amount Maxine inherited.

Maxine writes them a check on the spot, everybody signs the makeshift contract, Maxine and Brad proceed to hire a bunch of lawyers and investment guys, and pretty soon, "Once Upon A Dress" is franchised and booming. By the time Maxine learns that every night Brad takes their dog for a "long walk", he's stopping by an old flame for a rushed, nostalgic sexual encounter, the business is booming and about to be sold. The sale will make them zillionaires, just in time for the divorce proceedings.

The divorce goes on for *a decade*, as in, longer than it took to fight the Korean War. See, the thing about no-fault divorce, is that it really is *no fault*—who's a scum bag, or even who's the bigger scum bag, has nothing to do with who gets the money, or how much, or even what's fair. Equitable Division of property in divorce means just that: You consider everything financial that's happened during the marriage, and try to come up with an Even-Steven split of all the money and property built up throughout the marriage, *unless you have a Pre-Nup and the deal's been decided before you even got hitched.*

Maxine's and Brad's situation is *a mess*: Sure, the business was initially purchased with Maxine's inherited dough, but whose idea was it in the first place? Ideas that turn into money during the marriage can be *Marital Property,* subject to division in a divorce. And, even if Maxine had the first spark of inspiration, things were happening pretty fast that night in the shop, and Brad did haggle out that back-of-the-envelope contract, and then the value appreciated during the marriage, based on both of their efforts, and *uugghhh*, that's what this process is like. Sort of a mix of archaeology, accounting, detective work, knife-in-the-teeth combat and fingernails-in-the-ceiling arguing, that takes *years* to sort out.

With a Pre-Nup, Maxine could have made it legally binding so that everything bought with her pre-marital bonus and inherited money stayed her separate property—property she'd keep, in the event of divorce. Half the time, though, when lawyers give this advice, the response is something like, "It just seems so *unromantic.*"

True enough, and I'm sure Brad's ex-spouse and the kids from his first marriage appreciate their newly improved lifestyles, fueled by Brad's divorce-booty millions, so they'd advise against doing a Pre-Nup, too.....

8. NOT-SO-SECRET AGENTS: GUARDIANS AND GUARDIANSHIP

Suppose you wake up one morning, and all you can say is "Yes". You don't know it, but you've had a mild stroke. You still feel good, you're functional, able to walk around and you have all your marbles, but something happened in your sleep, so that when you try to talk, only "Yes" comes out, and when you try to write, all you can do is barely sign your name. You wander out the door and try to live your life, but right away, you start getting into trouble. You go to a restaurant and the manager thinks he recognizes you as the guy who reserved a room for a party. "Hey, Mr. Smith, your room for the special party of fifty is all set. We'll just put it on the credit card you used last month." You bring your car in for service, and the salesman says, "Oh, Smith, trading in your car for this new, super-expensive sporty thing? I got the paperwork ready for you to sign," and all you can do when you try to communicate is to say "Yes" and sign your name.

By the end of the first week, you're in deep water—you're in debt to just about everybody and you can't keep your job, so even if you wanted all the stuff you unintentionally bought being a Yes-Man, you couldn't begin to pay for it all.

You'd want somebody to step in and stop this, somebody to protect you from financial ruin.

Now, suppose just such a person arrives at your doorstep, an unwavering advocate who can run around behind you and rip up all those contracts you're signing and undo those agreements you're racking up by unintentionally saying "Yes" every time somebody tries to sell you something. Problem is, the only way you can get this person's help is to publicly admit something's wrong, so the law will give this new helper the right to tear up those restaurant bills and car purchases.

Do you let your fear of publicly acknowledging your problems interfere with your opportunity to set things straight?

Sounds like science fiction, but actually, I've pretty much described what happens in a *Guardianship.*

Guardianship, or *Conservatorship,* or *Protected Person's Estates* (the name varies state-to-state) is what happens when a disabled person, usually an elderly disabled person, has money and property that needs protecting. Probate Courts make a determination that you can't take care of yourself (then, you get a *Guardian of the Person)* or you can't manage your property (then, you get a *Guardian of the Estate* or *Conservator*), and the court appoints somebody, often a family member, a bank or social service agency, to do the taking-care. That estate guardian collects and invests the property, spends it pursuant to court supervision, and prevents you from unwittingly buying those sports cars and dinners for fifty. If it's a personal guardianship, the guardian makes sure you have the caregivers you need, and can place you in a custodial care setting if need be.

Know what the best thing is about *Guardianship?* Suppose Yes-Man already had a guardian. Now, imagine that salesman, trying to sell my Yes-Man that hundred-thousand-dollar sports car. All Yes-Man had to do was sign his name, so he seemed OK as he drove away. Car guy figures he's made a deal and earned a commission. Well, too bad for him. Those guardianship court files are a matter of public record. The salesman could have gone down to the courthouse, filled out a file request at the Court Clerk's Office and found out Yes-Man was an adjudicated disabled person, so the Law engages in the fiction that the salesman, and everybody else, did just that before making the sale, even though that *never* happens. The entire World is on what the law calls *Constructive Notice* that Yes-Man is disabled and has a guardian, meaning we'll all pretend everybody reads those court files, even though probate lawyers and the Court's file clerks are the only people who ever get close enough to those files to even *smell* them. That constructive notice is a message to the World not to mess with Yes-Man, so his guardian gets to waltz into that car dealership and rip up that contract, with no cost to Yes-Man, even if he's put a few miles on the car.

And, there's more: If the guardian is a human, they need to be bonded, meaning he or she has an insurance policy backing them up so that if the guardian goes rogue and rips you off or exceeds court authority and it costs you money, you're still covered for any loss. As an extra, added bonus, you get this: Guardianship judges are notorious for nickel and diming guardians and their lawyers, shredding their fees and keeping them on a short leash, only allowing them to spend your money on a transaction-by-transaction basis, each time only after the Guardian asks the Court for permission.

So, why does everybody hate Guardianship so much?

Guardianship is the most vilified thing probate courts and lawyers do. Whenever I suggest to somebody with a family member badly in need of Guardianship that they obtain a doctor's report, the first step to getting disabled person status, they recoil and launch into invective.

"Mom would have *hated* this."

Really? You talked to Mom about going to court so you could save her from the poorhouse, and she said, "Let it all *burn?*"

"Dad would never have wanted the whole world to know about his Alzheimer's Disease."

You don't say? In over forty years of handling over a hundred guardianships, I've never had *anybody,* let alone a reporter, copy and publicize a single page from guardianship court files, and I've never drawn a single phone call from the press about a guardianship under administration.

Guardianship is one of the most unfairly maligned legal proceedings in the World—distressed, privacy-obsessed family members project their own concerns on their elderly, disabled family members, who could care less. Meanwhile, they get themselves into a lot of trouble, waiting to go to court to protect disabled relatives until it's too late. You're asking, *Too late for what?* Too late to freeze out the crooked caregiver who's slipping notes to Gramps to sign, changing his accounts to joint tenancy with the caregiver; too late to frustrate your unctuous brother Phil, who wheedles his way into Mom's condo with *his* lawyer in tow, getting Mom to sign that codicil (an amendment to her will) or trust amendment giving Phil control over everything when Mom dies.

Guardianship is a pain in the ass for the Guardians and lawyers who deal with it—the record keeping requirements are horrendous, and everything requires a trip to court for which you can never get fully compensated. That said, it's relatively painless for the people it's protecting. They are never in the courtroom, unless there's a fight over whether they *need* a guardian, which is rare. Their money and property are hyper-protected, and all close calls go to the disabled person, meaning any time somebody claims the disabled person owes them money, they are going to lose.

Nonetheless, people avoid it like *the plague*, and as a consequence, elderly folks get ripped off a lot.

The Wheelchair, The Bus Stop and Fifteen Social Security Numbers

Jane is the oldest of five children of her elderly father Bert, who's wheelchair-bound and slightly losing it. Bert has lots of money and his estate plan is in order. The carefully drafted trusts that govern ownership of his assets, meticulously split up control between all five children's family lines. It's a scheme that insures all the kids will continue to benefit equally from his estate, which supports them all while it supports Dad as well.

Sounds ideal and tranquil, and for a while it is, but there's always one jerk in a crowd this big, and in this case it's third child Max, who believes he should run the estate and deserves a bigger share of the pie than his siblings. Daughter Jane is worried Max will do something bad, because Max has hired his own lawyer, who Max claims has some "ideas", designed to help elderly father Bert save taxes. She sees Max coming and going from Dad's condo a lot these days, but she's not panicking yet because Bert has round-the-clock nurses, who, Jane is certain, would alert her if anything fishy was happening.

Jane's lawyer advises her to consider getting guardianship over elderly father Bert, as he'd never know the difference or care. Guardianship would render anything brother Max did to upset Bert's long-time plan "presumptively void", lawyer talk for not worth the paper it's written on.

"Dad would hate Guardianship," she tells lawyer.

"I hear that a lot," lawyer tells her.

It doesn't take long for circumstances to prove her lawyer right. Weeks later, Jane comes to her lawyer's office all charged up, accompanied by one of her father's care-giver nurses, who's in tears. When her lawyer asks the nurse to tell him what happened, she's *sobbing*, mascara running down the face and onto her neck, can't-wipe-it-away-fast-enough *sobbing*. When a witness can't recount events without going through an entire box of Kleenex, it's a sure sign you should sit up and take notes, so this is *serious*.

Seems brother Max showed up at Dad's condo with Max's own lawyer as a sidekick, demanding Father sign a bunch of new documents Max's attorney has prepared, which would give Max control of all Dad's property, including two businesses Dad started but no longer runs. Father is pretty out of it, but has a few marbles left, doesn't particularly like or trust Max, has never seen Max's lawyer before, and anyway, his morning routine usually just consists of getting spoon fed breakfast and then watching television with the nurse. When Bert reflexively refuses to sign anything, Max loses it and starts yelling.

With one of the nurses pounding on Max's back, Max grabbed the handles of Dad's wheelchair and ran with it, out of the condo, into the elevator and out to the sidewalk.

"You're 'gonna be out in the *street!*" Max was shouting, as he literally pushed Bert and his wheelchair out over the curb. Father's building sits at the corner of a busy thoroughfare, which is the site a high-traffic bus stop. The nurse reports that she was still clinging to Max and shouting, occasionally landing a fist on Max's back, as Max shoved father's wheelchair into the street, with Dad nearly falling out.

"This is what's 'gonna happen to you: Out on the *street!*" Max screamed, as a bus pulled in and stopped just short of flattening them.

So Bert, tears streaming down *his* face, wordlessly reached for the pen and sitting at the bus stop, he methodically signed the documents Max's lawyer handed him.

Jane stops the nurse's story to add, "Those were amendments to Dad's trust that put Max in control of everything—he's telling us he's cutting our distributions and threatening to cut out my sister. He's already tripled his own distributions from Dad's trusts."

"Perhaps we should go for that guardianship," Jane's lawyer suggests, seems to him, like, for the *forty-third time.* "We could set aside all those documents, which were clearly signed under duress."

"I couldn't do that to Dad—he'd hate it," Jane refuses, yet again.

Meanwhile, brother Max hires an out-of-work, thirty-five-year-old, on-the-skids actress to be his eyes and ears in the condo. He introduces Actress/Fake Nurse to Dad as just another nurse. Since he now has control over the purse strings, he works Actress/Fake Nurse into Bert's daily schedule, and Actress/Fake Nurse begins to notice the huge balances on the financial account statements she sees lying around the condo. Pretty soon, Bert has made a substantial "gift" to Actress/Fake Nurse.

"Now we *really* need to go for guardianship," Jane's lawyer advises. "We can exercise some badly-needed control over who comes and goes from that condo."

You guessed right. "I just can't do that to Dad," Jane says in tears, now competing with Bert's real nurse for the Full-Box-of-Kleenex award.

While Jane dithers about the indignities of guardianship, Actress/Fake Nurse turns out to be even more aggressive and conniving than Max. She's busy collecting all those financial account statements from Bert's many bank and brokerage accounts, which arrive at the Condo monthly. One-by-one, she is sticking transfer documents in front of Bert, having him sign forms and methodically transferring the accounts into her name. When Max finds out he is outraged, mostly because Actress/Fake Nurse beat him to the punch.

Now Jane wants to go for guardianship, which she does—she gets appointed guardian of Bert's property and person, and proceeds to sue the daylights out of Actress/Fake Nurse, and, while she's at it, she sues Max, too. Actress/Fake Nurse has used fifteen different social security numbers to set up the transferred accounts, with vaguely similar aliases associated with each phony number. The unwinding therefore takes forever, Bert dies in the meantime, and post-death litigation ensues, which costs a fortune.

When it's over, Jane and her other siblings have prevailed over Max and Actress/Fake Nurse, but Jane's lawyer has essentially become an equal partner in the enterprise, given how much they've had to pay him.

"Tell me the truth," Jane asks her lawyer. "How much would it have cost if we'd just gone for guardianship in the first place?"

"I don't know......peanuts, comparatively," lawyer has to confess.

Then, there's guardianships for kids, *minors*, as they're called here.

The thing is, kids, like dead people, can't own stuff, at least, not until they're eighteen. Parents can't actually sign legal documents and receive money for those child actors, teen-age inventors creating video games in their basements and kids who inherit money. No, contrary to the most common misconception in the realm of legal folk-wisdom, parents cannot bind their kids in contracts or transact business for them, *simply because they are their parents*. You need to be appointed Guardian by a court to even open up accounts and register property for your kids, if it is actually their stuff.

This is different from those custody accounts that are legally really in the parents' names, the way most people open teeny bank accounts for their kids with Christmas money from grandma. In formal, minors' Guardianships, you need to get bonded (more insurance) and account to the court annually, as Guardian of the Estate of your kids. Even then, you can't do anything without asking the court *each time* you want to sign something with financial consequences for your kids, like booking them into that photo shoot for the amusement park advertising campaign.

This, too, is not an accident. There's a reason for all this, and that reason is Charlie Chaplin. That's right—*that* Charlie Chaplin, the Little Tramp, the silent film star—he's the reason you need formal, court-appointed guardianship to get control of money owed to or belonging to your kids.

Chaplin made a film in 1921, his first feature longer than a two-reeler, a movie called *The Kid*. Chaplin plays a window installer who wanders the streets offering to replace broken windows, carrying the replacements on his back. It's a scam: A little street urchin, a cute kid of about six who teams up with Chaplin, runs around ahead of him throwing bricks through peoples' windows, so Chaplin will have customers who need his windows.

The film was wildly successful and the kid was played by a child actor named Jackie Coogan. Coogan made a bundle, but he got ripped off by his mother and stepfather, who were "managing" the hundreds of thousands he made as a child actor, back when that was really a lot of money. They blew through most of it, which they were able to get their hands on because in the 1920's, parents were able to contract for their kids without court supervision in most states. Californians were so stunned by the ensuing scandal that they passed a series of laws that required formal guardianship for handling kid money like child-actor fees, and soon the rest of the country followed suit.

Guardianship for kids is much like it is for adults, except that it ends abruptly when the kid turns eighteen, unless the kid got the money for being disabled, like a medical malpractice or birth trauma case. Then, the kid becomes a disabled adult at eighteen and gets a disabled-adult guardian. Most parents don't think an eighteen-year-old is any better qualified to handle money than a seventeen-year-old. Well, too bad: Writing the kid a check for all that guardianship money, a check the kid is free to blow, is what's going to happen at the eighteenth birthday, the formal end of minor guardianship. Again, this is one of those problems that can be addressed with an attorney. An experienced probate lawyer has trusts and other options that your eighteen-year-old may find acceptable as a place to safeguard the money at eighteen, and those options may save the kid from buying a motorcycle with the dough, or getting ripped off by her drug-addled friends.

What's tough to deal with during Minors' Guardianships is the Court acting like Scrooge with the money. Unless your kid is a child actor or childhood software programming prodigy, these guardianship funds most often arise from infant birth trauma or child-injury lawsuit recoveries. That means the kid will likely need the money the rest of his or her life, so the courts view their role as gatekeeper in a struggle to protect the multi-million-dollar settlement fund from the very human attempt by the rest of the family to share the wealth. Typically, the recovery makes the injured child a millionaire, while the siblings and parents are regular folks, just struggling to make ends meet.

Family members often hate minors' guardianships because the probate judge watches the money like a hawk, essentially assuming, without expressly saying so, that the parents are potential crooks. The court is trying to resist the outcome where the kid doesn't have enough money, throughout his or her life, to maintain medical and care-giving needs. This is balanced against the parents' lobbying to buy a larger house, ostensibly for the disabled child, where, of course, the parents and the siblings will also live. Probate courts also frequently deal with requests to pay one of the disabled child's parents a "fee" for acting as "caregiver" for the child, typically a thinly-veiled attempt to improve overall family lifestyle using the injured kid's money.

Don't shy away from minor guardianship just because it may seem like the Court is assuming you're a freeloader trying to rip off your kid's money: They *need* to assume everybody's a schnook. The Court's job is to police the very human tendency to smoosh together what parents think of as the best interests of the child, with their own, self-centered desires. It's not *you* as a particular parent they're targeting—they *constructively* have to indiscriminately suspect all parents and siblings of greedy self-interest. The Court will usually end up letting you buy a nice house with the dough, and allow the entire family to live there rent-free with the injured kid, because even though they're supposed to faithfully protect the kid's money, they don't want the rest of the family to end up resenting the wealthy kid with the big estate.

Like everything else in this process, guardianship is only a pain in the ass because the alternative—having kids ripped off—is much, much worse.

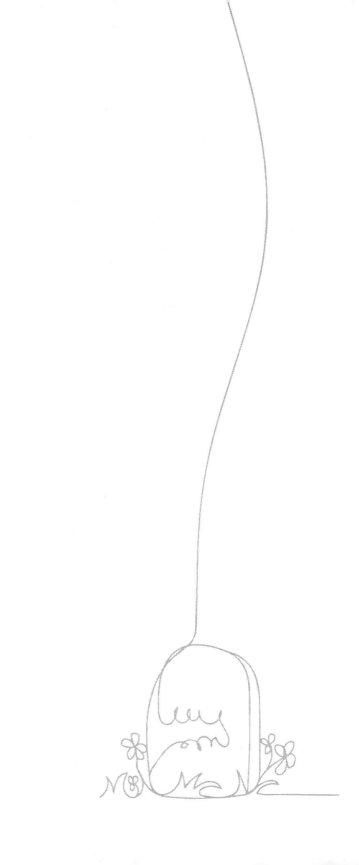

9. DEATH BY NOTARY: POWERS OF ATTORNEY FOR PROPERTY AND HEALTH CARE, AND LIVING WILLS

Now that I've cured you of your guardianship phobia, let's talk about something often used (or, in my opinion, overused) as a popular guardianship antidote: *Powers of Attorney.*

Remember those scary joint tenancies in Chapter Two, where you sort of vaguely recollected signing a little card at your bank, but then all of a sudden somebody starts raiding your bank account and walks away with all your property at your death?

Now suppose you signed some forms at your lawyer's office that you barely understood, but they looked official, had lots of fine print and got notarized by your lawyer's secretary, using this very important-looking stamp that made her seem like the Governor, or at least, a member of Congress. What if it turns out that, unbeknownst to you, those forms gave somebody the right to grab *all your property*, run away with it, and if you land in the hospital without all your cylinders firing, *pull the plug on your life support*?

Welcome to *Powers of Attorney*, the scariest documents in a probate lawyer's bag of tricks. Powers of Attorney are the most over-prescribed and poorly understood legal instruments since the advent of mandatory arbitration clauses in automobile purchase contracts.

Powers of Attorney are essentially *agency* agreements, forms that appoint somebody to do things for you and when those agents do things, those acts have the same legal impact as acts you do yourself. Powers of Attorney name somebody as your stand-in and come in two varieties: Property and Health Care. Property powers give that agent power to make deals for you, spend your money, move your money around from account to account, buy and sell your stuff, even sign other legal documents, like trusts. Health Care powers give your agent authority to make medical decisions for you, like consent to surgery, administer medication or even terminate life support if you can't live without things like respirators or feeding tubes.

While your lawyer may have his or her own forms for these powers, increasingly lawyers (and, do-it-yourselfers) use official, state-sponsored forms that track language in the laws that make Powers of Attorney enforceable. This means your bank and your broker are supposed to follow directions when your agent shows up and says, "Do something with this person's money because *I said so*." Lawyers use these official forms because they are more likely than homemade forms to get *accepted*, or acted upon by the banks and hospitals.

Once upon a time, Powers of Attorney were only good, meaning effective to authorize your agent to do stuff, as long as you were fully competent. The idea was that so long as you could yank the power by ripping it up and telling your agent to knock it off, it was OK to let people run around armed with these extremely powerful documents. Lawyers and others came to realize that most people would also want these powers to remain effective once they'd lost their marbles, since many people were using these as guardianship substitutes— giving people powers that your agents could then use to cash checks and pay bills, once you were too out of it to do that yourself.

The result of this sensitivity to disability planning was a series of laws in the 1980's and 1990's, which, in most states, rendered powers of attorney *durable*, meaning they'd continue to be effective until you die, no matter how cognitively blasted you might become. Like a lot of well-intended legal developments, this one had both good and bad consequences. The good: A simple form you sign as a routine matter at that meeting when you executed your will, could give your spouse or your kids a way of dealing with your stuff and directing your doctors without your help or without your even knowing about it—valuable powers when you're losing it. The bad: The same form could give your spouse or your kids, or *just about anybody else*, the power to do just about anything with you and your stuff, even if those people were up to no good. Today, most Powers of Attorney executed, especially those that use official, state-sponsored pre-printed forms, are *durable* –they operate when you're disabled—unless you specifically modify them, which almost nobody does.

If that sounds like powers of attorney are a little scary, that's because *they are*. I see no reason to sugarcoat it: In the wrong hands, Powers of Attorney can be dangerous, destructive tools for bad people to do bad things to you, your person and your stuff.

Who, then, are the *right* hands? I'm probably going to get hate mail over this, but:

- Only spouses should generally be designated agent in a Property Power of Attorney; and

- Only spouses, or, *if you don't have a spouse*, an adult child, should be designated agent in a Health Care Power of Attorney, *but only if that child can be trusted with your life*.

And, when I say spouses (here comes more hate mail), I mean first spouses, spouses who are the parent of at least one of your children, if you have any, or a spouse you can trust, if your kids are trying to get your money—generally not that fourth spouse who is thirty-five years younger than you are and is constantly fighting with your kids, who happen to be older than he or she is.

Why? The only person who should have the power to do just about anything you can do with your stuff should be the person you most trust, and also somebody who has little incentive to misuse the Property Power of Attorney, *because he or she is getting most of your property someday anyway.* For most people, that's your spouse, unless you're on number four and he or she has a straight-jacket pre-nup that says they get nothing at your death. If that's you, then, time to turn to the kids.

The only person who should be able to pull the plug on your life support as agent under your Health Care Power should be your spouse, who you hopefully trust, but even in a less-than-perfect world where you sort-of trust your spouse, a spouse who stands to have his her or life most disrupted if you kick the bucket unexpectedly. If there is no spouse in the picture, then a child whose personal attachment outweighs any greed or resentment factor, should be agent under your Health Care Power. And, in all cases, that child should be somebody who does not need or want your money.

Am I overreacting?

Good Thing We Didn't Cancel His Subscription to *Sports Illustrated*

Laura is married to Peter, an engineer who makes bundles designing power plants. It's her first marriage, his second and she's ten years younger. Peter has four kids from a prior marriage, and they all don't exactly get along—the kids wore black armbands to the wedding and held a mock funeral on Peter and Laura's front lawn after their wedding reception.

Peter is in his sixties and has a history of high blood pressure. One day at work he inexplicably passes out and is rushed to the hospital. By the time Laura gets there, he's in a coma and two of his kids, Betty and Ralph, are circling his hospital bed, barking orders at the nurses. They attempt to throw Laura out of the room, flashing a Health Care Power of Attorney naming them co-agents, one that Peter signed years before the marriage and apparently never tore up or *revoked.*

They are insisting the nurses flag Peter's bedside chart with a *DNR* order, or *Do Not Resuscitate,* basically telling the staff to let Peter die if anything bad happens, not to take any extraordinary measures to keep him alive. They claim the authority to demand this because of that Health Care Power, which, however old it may be, is still *durable,* hanging around and effective, even though Peter is out of it.

Laura goes to probate court and gets appointed Peter's guardian, after an emergency trial in which she testifies she's discussed end-of-life decisions with Peter and he'd want all possible measures taken to prolong his life in his current situation. Her lawyer then commences a second lawsuit—that's right, *two* trials are needed—to try to convince the court that the kids are misusing the Power. The lawyer argues the kids are acting against Peter's declared wishes to live, *no matter what,* even if he thoughtlessly or mistakenly checked the wrong box on the Power of Attorney he gave the kids years ago. That little fine-print box on the form says: "Do not unnecessarily prolong my life if the potential quality of my continued life will be outweighed by the expense and burden on others of such continued life."

A lengthy trial ensues, with conflicting medical testimony about just how fried Peter's brain may be, since, like with a lot of coma patients, the doctors cannot exactly predict the likelihood of recovery, or the extent of brain damage. "Miracles do happen," one doctor testifies, as he shrugs his shoulders.

Laura's lawyer is fighting to get Peter's financial records that the kids are hiding, on the theory that you always follow the money in these cases, but the kids refuse to surrender any financial documents. Laura's lawyer persists, because as long as the trial is proceeding, the probate judge has blocked the DNR order and directed the hospital staff to keep Peter alive.

During the second month of the trial, Peter suddenly awakens from the coma and asks for an egg salad sandwich. After a wobbly week, he seems mostly recovered, but Laura's attorney doesn't let go of the attempt to invalidate the Power; Laura does not want a repeat performance if this happens again.

Sure enough, when Laura's attorney finally gets the financial documents, it turns out Peter also has an old, out-of-date will, signed years before he married Laura. That outdated will leaves everything to the kids, with nothing for Laura, who he hadn't even met when he signed that will. The kids' true motivation in trying to pull the plug on Peter was their concern that, if he was revived, Peter would get around to executing a new will, where he'd cut the kids out of his estate, leaving everything to Laura.

Lawyers tend to hand Powers of Attorney out like gumdrops these days. Some attorneys will even assume they've dropped the ball if they don't get powers signed up with the will and trust execution. Sorry, but not everybody needs Powers of Attorney. There's always guardianship if something needs doing and the person is too out of it to give direction. I know, I know—you're not convinced by my previous chapter that guardianship's such a great thing after all, and Powers of Attorney only add a couple hundred dollars to the lawyer's bill when you get your will and trust drafted, so why not sign powers?

First, if you're worried about mischief so you revoke a Power of Attorney, you still need to warn off any third parties like your bank, before they act on a direction by your agent under that Power. The bank may be moving money around based on the power, and if you don't get to them before they pay a bill or empty your account, it's your tough luck—they're protected unless you can prove they had *actual notice* that the Power of Attorney had been revoked by you. Worse yet, in most states, the bank is also protected even if the Power of Attorney is a fake or forged, unless they have *actual notice* that it's a forgery.

Second, while a Guardian can get appointed and go to court to challenge both the validity of the Power itself and the specific action being taken, those lawsuits are some of the most complex, protracted and emotionally draining experiences for everybody, including the Judge, when it's a Health Care Power and your life's on the line. Worse yet, in some states, there's a circular problem to even getting such lawsuits off the ground—you often can't get a Guardian appointed in the first place to even begin a court challenge to the Power of Attorney, unless you can show that the Power of Attorney is being abused by the Agent. Even if you get a guardian, the case still comes down to abuse of the power, not just a disagreement over medical treatment.

"Abuse", in this case, means more than just you disagree with the actions being taken. To have the court block a renegade agent from misusing the power, you typically need to show that the agent is causing substantial harm, "in a manner not authorized or intended" under the power. That's right: It's not enough to go to court and prove, "The agent is *killing* Dad," you need to also prove that, "The agent is killing Dad in a way *not intended* by Dad." That's a much tougher case to win than, "Wait a second, Judge—I think he'd want to live, under the circumstances." So, a meandering court hearing plays out with a bunch of testimony about whether you *really, badly*, wanted to die, in the circumstance of just this set of medical maladies, while the feeding tube to your belly slowly drip-drip-drips.

Scared, yet? If the same case comes to guardianship court with no Power of Attorney mucking up the trial, it's just a question of whether you'd be better off alive than dead. Yeah, I'll take my chances on meeting *that* standard.

So, if you're going to sign one of these things, keep these pointers in mind:

- Health Care Powers are fairly confusing, if you actually read them. There are lots of choices to make about when, whether and under what circumstances to discontinue life support, so make your lawyer explain *all of them*. Usually, if you don't mark up the power, you're giving your agent the power to kill you, no matter what.

- People think you need to grant the agent all the powers listed, but you can trim back the scope of any Power of Attorney to something less than everything listed in the form. Don't be shy about crossing stuff out.

- Most Powers contain a guardianship designation, a place where you can pick who gets to be guardian, if you need one. Pick somebody—the fight in guardianship litigation is usually over *who* gets to *be* Guardian, not whether somebody *needs* a Guardian. Your designated guardian will usually get to act, unless he or she is *unfit,* meaning a convicted felon or somebody who's lost their own marbles.

- Avoid two or more co-agents. As a seasoned probate judge once said to me: "I hate co-*anything*." He was talking about how co-agents always end up disagreeing and fighting. Then you need to go to court to break the tie, thus defeating one purpose of having the Power of Attorney in the first place.

- Make sure your lawyer keeps a signed, original of your Property Power, and your doctor keeps a signed, original of your Health Care Power. Sometimes these things need to be used in a hurry, so even if you've taken my advice and used a safe deposit box for your documents, you don't want family members locked out of the bank when you're unconscious and need open heart surgery.

Many states now have so-called "Health Care Proxies," or people who automatically have some of the powers of an agent under a Health Care Power, when you never got around to signing one. You should ask your probate lawyer if your state has these Proxies, but not because you want to rely on those Proxy rules. Health Care Proxies are "picked" for you by statute, usually close relatives, but the state's choices can often progress all the way down a list to "longtime friend or close acquaintance". In much the same way that you don't want the state picking your will beneficiaries with intestacy, you probably don't want the risk management officer at the hospital deciding who your "longtime friends and close acquaintances" may be, so they can pull your feeding tube. Ironically, the existence of these Health Care Proxy statutes is the best reason to have a Health Care Power of Attorney—at least with a power, *you* get to pick who decides whether to pull your plug.

How do *Living Wills* fit in?

Living Wills are much more limited in what they do than Health Care Powers. Living Wills are just statements of the extent you do, or do not, want extraordinary measures taken to keep you alive, usually only in the event a full recovery isn't possible. They were floated into the marketplace before most states had Health Care Powers, and are now used primarily in situations where Powers are not signed, but the person knows they don't want to be kept alive with apparatus like feeding tubes.

Living wills were originally created to deal with what is, in my opinion, a somewhat overblown concern that the living-will-maker would otherwise end up stranded long-term in a hospital in a permanent, vegetative state. While these cases do rarely occur, they are usually the product of religious issues or inter-family squabbles, and are better dealt with by a Health Care Power, which can authorize the agent to deal with *any* medical condition.

Keep in mind, the practical impact of having a Living Will is your hospital medical chart will be tagged with a DNR, a Do Not Resuscitate order. That means nobody you know, nobody you picked ahead of time, will be making the decision on whether to take extraordinary measures to keep you alive *at the moment of your immediate hospitalization*. That decision will be made by a medical provider, who will assume you want to die unless your outlook is rosy. So, before you sign a living will, you should carefully consider how you feel about the medical profession in general and miracle cures in particular, since you're effectively leaving the decision to keep you alive up to somebody you've never met. You may think you're a real charmer, but almost everybody looks and smells like a dead fish when they're unconscious.

10. CAN TRUSTS BE TRUSTED, AND, WHAT *IS* A TRUST, ANYWAY?

If you're one of those people that doesn't like to admit you don't understand things other people talk about casually, as though they were *born* with tech-familiarity, like *gigabytes* and *femtoseconds*, and exotic subjects such as trusts are like that for you, don't be embarrassed. Me too: In my first class on my first day of law school, my civil procedure professor started diagramming a complex structure on the blackboard, as he asked a question about a trust. The hypothetical had all sorts of Latin-sounding terms in it, like "Cestui Que Trust", and it involved some kind of big-money dispute.

I had no idea what he was talking about. I was sitting with a buddy of mine I'd known since college. His father was a house painter and his mother a secretary, so I figured he had about as much reason as I did to know anything about trusts, which sounded like some kind of big-money thing.

"I'll give you twenty bucks if you shout out, "What's a Trust?" I whispered.

Not taking the bait, my buddy whispered back, "I think it's when you give your money to somebody you trust."

While he was just guessing, turns out he wasn't too far off.

If you're one of those people who think *Trusts* sound kind of *sneaky*, nobody would blame you. After all, the very-scary-sounding *Anti-Trust Laws* were enacted to *bust-up* trusts, and that sounds bad, right? You bust up bad stuff, like illegal hooch stills in Kentucky and empty cardboard boxes, mucking up your garage.

Turns out, trusts are actually pretty benign, and they were initially created long ago for the noblest of reasons—even if they've grown complicated and are sometimes used these days for seemingly sinister purposes. Trusts can even be understood, if, like me, you're a slow learner and you take it in small steps.

When you own stuff, you can do all sorts of things with it: You can sell it, you can play with it, you can live on it, you can rent it to somebody and you can borrow money and use it to back up your debts. The reasons you can do all these things are twofold: You have *Title* to your property, the legal registration that proves you own it and can fight off other people if they try to take it; and you have the *Beneficial Interest* in your property, the right to use it, exploit it and do fun and profitable stuff with it, for your endless enjoyment.

Suppose you were a rich guy in Merry Old England in the good old days (and, to be rich, you would have been *a guy* back then, who got your lands from the King). Suppose you were going around the world to fight in some crusade, riding off to some hardscrabble corner of the Middle East to look for a religious artifact or convert some unruly Pagans to the King's religion. Suppose you wanted to leave your stuff with somebody reputable who could watch over it and let your womenfolk still enjoy the benefits of ownership, like private, hot-water bathtubs and a guarded moat to prevent the womenfolk from getting kidnapped in their sleep. The Chancellor of the Exchequer, one of the King's official big shots, was empowered to serve just such a function, and trusts were born.

A trust is created when you transfer title to your property to somebody, a *Trustee,* not to absolutely own it, like when you sell your house or trade in a used car, but just to manage it for the benefit of yet another person, the *Beneficiary* of the trust you just created. That beneficiary gets to *use* the property for all that good stuff, like living on it if it's land or spending it if it's money. A trust document spells out how this arrangement is supposed to work, and most importantly when, if ever, the beneficiary, or his or her kids or grandkids or great grandkids, are supposed to actually get the money free of that trust. The trust document has a lot of other provisions, but at its heart, it tells you how long the trust will last and who gets money, in the meantime and at the end.

There are a million different kinds of trusts and they're used for a million different reasons, but virtually all trusts are created, at least in part, to do two things: Minimize taxes and exercise some control over property you don't want the beneficiaries, the people who are living it up on that property, to control themselves.

Sounds like rich-people stuff, and often it is, so I'll leave the fancy stuff to the high-octane lawyers, and just focus here on what every average American citizen should know about trusts.

Trusts used by ordinary humans, anybody not trying to set up perpetual, multi-billion-dollar empires of sprawling portfolios full of operating businesses and real estate, generally fall into three categories: *Revocable Trusts,* trusts that don't do much until your death and are used with your will as a part of your post-death plan; *Irrevocable Gift Trusts,* which take effect as soon as you sign them and are designed primarily to escape taxes on whatever you put in them; and *Minor's Trusts,* often more modest arrangements meant to hold property set aside for young people until they get old enough not to blow it all.

Most people don't have enough money to seriously invest in an *Irrevocable Gift Trust*, since you, personally, need to be hands-off whatever you put in there for the rest of your life to make it work. The idea is you park money or other property there that's not worth much, then it grows tax free and the income dribbles out to your kids and grandkids over time, escaping wealth taxes at your death because you already gave it away. Eventually, your remote descendants, like great-grandkids, get a bonanza when the trust terminates and a whopping amount is distributed to them.

For the last 12 years, the tax laws have made this sort of trust-related tax planning silly for most people with family wealth under ten million (more about that later), but people still love these things, so let's just say this: Since most people can't afford to park anything of value in an irrevocable gift trust for the rest of their lives, these trusts tend to only get used by most ordinary humans as vehicles for holding life insurance.

When you transfer a life insurance policy into an irrevocable gift trust, it's called an *Irrevocable Life Insurance Trust or ILIT*, (pronounced like *eyelid*, so now you know what your neighbors are talking about at your next party when you overhear, "We set up a bunch of *eyelids* for the kids"). Doing this is affordable, because the growth, at least in theory, comes from paying relatively modest insurance premiums to support the policy, which will then explode in value, tax-free, when you die. Then, all that money is parked in a trust that was worth peanuts when you set it up, and any wealth tax was assessed back then on those peanuts. These trusts are not for everybody, though, since you need to keep up the insurance premiums, and there are strict reporting and bookkeeping rules. My advice: skip these things unless you want to maintain a mega-sized, term life insurance policy (See Chapter 11), and then go to a lawyer and follow the technical advice on how to run an ILIT. It's fairly complicated, and unless you have more than eleven million personal net worth, probably unnecessary, unless you too want some money gossip for your next party.

Minor's Trusts are also a bit of overkill for typical folks, unless again, you're doing well enough to put a six-figure amount away for your kids while they're babies, and kiss it goodbye. Since you create these for the same wealth-tax leveraging reason—put the money in as peanuts (less than fifteen grand a year), and whatever it grows to passes tax-free to the kids—the same, "No-touch" rule applies to these trusts. There's no dipping in for you or even for the kids, because as long as they are minors, spending the trust on them—even having the power to spend it on them for basic support—has the same bad tax consequences as if you grabbed the money and spent it yourself. That causes the trust to be taxed at your death, just like you still own it. The only way to avoid that result is to have a non-parent act as trustee, with no power to pay for your kids' day-to-day expenses you'd be obligated to pay—often not an easy choice.

Minor's trusts are designed to receive these wealth-tax-free gifts to minors, and the only real advantage they offer over custodial accounts, simple bank accounts you manage for gifts to your kids, is that your minor's trusts can hold the property in trust past the time when the kid reaches twenty-one. There are complicated notice rules, though, and like all trusts there are record keeping requirements, investment guidelines and tax returns to be filed. Again, I'd skip these and use so-called Uniform Transfers to Minors' Custody Accounts for kid-money. If, on the other hand, you've got a hundred thousand smackers to put in trust for your kids, money you're never going to need again, and you expect to become uber-wealthy someday, then you can justify paying a lawyer to draft a minor's trust and sort out the follow up.

However, CONSUMER WARNING: See Chapter 20, about the pitfalls of giving your kids money before they are as old and crusty as you are.

That leaves us with *Revocable Trusts*, usually executed simultaneously with your will. Even for people in the peanuts to million-dollar range, these are a pretty good idea, and most lawyers will suggest them to operate in tandem with your will. The standard design is that your will states that the residue of your estate, what's left over after specific gifts of items like vehicles, jewelry and furniture, gets "poured over", or transferred to your revocable trust. That revocable trust then contains the guts of your post-death plan, the who-gets-what part, which can include outright gifts of property at your death, or provisions that keep the property tied up for years, just like those long-term gift trusts you were too poor to set up during life.

Now you're dead, so you don't need to personally dip in to the property anymore, so now you can "afford" a trust. Holding property up with a trustee managing it for your kids and grandkids might make more sense than giving it to them outright. This is no longer tax driven: If your revocable trust continues to hold property past your death, it's usually because you don't want your kids blowing it all on silly investments, motorcycles and bad marriages. The convenient thing about it, though, is that this trust document didn't get locked in until your death, so, like your will, you could change it anytime until you died.

I generally think most folks should have one of these revocable trusts, even though you can pretty much provide for the same post-death plans in your will as you would in a revocable trust. So, then, why ask your lawyer to draft two documents when one will do?

These are the advantages of having a revocable trust that can't be duplicated with will-only planning:

- Their provisions are private, as they don't get filed with the court (in most States) at death the way your will does;

- You can *fund* them during your life, i.e., transfer your property into one while you're still alive, avoiding guardianship if you become disabled;

- They can be updated on a simple, single signature (yours), as they don't need to be witnessed (in most states) in a formal execution ceremony like wills do; and

- They allow for more flexible, post-death investment and administration than estates governed by your will.

I know, right about now, you're thinking, "Wait a minute! He just said guardianship was a *good* thing, so why is side-stepping guardianship with a living trust you transfer your property into before you die, why is that a good thing?"

Guardianship's great when you need it to protect an elderly person from getting ripped off or sign up a child actor for a well-paying commercial gig. If the only reason you need guardianship is because somebody's no longer able to sign things or balance a checkbook, a guardianship is a lot of work, just to be able to pay somebody's bills (Somebody who wisely took my advice and didn't give a power of attorney to his cousin Herbie or his sixth spouse). If you're over fifty-five, when strokes become a bigger risk, and you've signed a revocable trust as part of your planning for death, a successor trustee named in the trust document can step in for you and manage your property without court involvement if you become disabled.

This manage-my-stuff-if-I-become-disabled feature just requires that you *fund the trust*, meaning retitle your accounts and other property to "Mr. Smith, as Trustee of the Mr. Smith Trust", and just like that, you've successfully avoided guardianship. This will also prevent the financial abuses that might otherwise drive you into guardianship, as your successor trustee can protect your accounts from mayhem, because she (or a bank) takes over automatically if you've lost your capacity.

I suggest life-time trust funding to over-age-fifty-five clients with virtually any size estate, with one word of caution: You need to do this re-registration with *everything*, and that includes the checking account you use at the grocery store and the dentist's office. Otherwise, if you become disabled, your successor trustee can't get access to the assets and accounts still listed in your name, and you need guardianship or a dreaded power of attorney for those.

This aspect, having your day-to-day checking account registered to your trust, weirds people out. If you ask, Banks will hide trustee ownership on your checks, so the checks themselves *don't* say, "John Smith, as Trustee of the Smith Trust....." in the address block on the checks. Do this. Otherwise, the folks standing behind you in the grocery store check-out line will see a trustee registration on your checks, and assume you are either: 1. A Jerk; or 2. Rich. The latter is not a good thing, particularly if the guy in line behind you is a drunk buying himself a quart.

So, then, if just about everybody who gets a post-death plan should have a living trust, what's gives trusts a bad name?

In a word: *Duration.*

There's this bargain-basement, printing-press industry of do-it-yourself trust mongering, where self-help enthusiasts hand out single page trust forms, and offer seminars at the local Holiday Inn about how to set up these *Dynasty Trusts*. Fill out the form, transfer a few bucks to yourself as trustee, and, *violá,* you've got a little chugger *that goes on nearly forever.*

Trusts were not originally designed to go on forever. Since those good old days British folks who created trusts let the cat out of the bag, trusts have been governed by something called, "The Rule Against Perpetuities", a bit of legal gobbledygook that is lawyer talk for, "Don't go on longer than about one hundred years". Trusts governed by this rule, which is still most trusts, end around a hundred years after execution, whether you like it or not and tried to say otherwise in the trust document. At that hundred-year deadline, the trusts end, and the property held by the trustee gets handed out to whichever relative of yours is still around to get the booty, usually grandchildren or great grandchildren.

Under pressure from people with real money, states have begun loosening or abolishing this rule, so more and more states allow you to set up perpetual trusts. That's right: Even if you only put $5,000 in the trust account, the document can now say the money gets held up *forever*. The carnival-barker allure of these things is the false promise that they will grow to enormity over the millennium, and your great-great-great-great grandchildren's children will live like the Rockefellers. This is silly nonsense for a number of reasons, the main one being that generations multiply faster and more prolifically than money grows, and administration expenses eat into the value in those early years before your $5,000 has a chance to turn into billions. The do-it-yourselfers are convincing just plain people to set up these pretend dynasty builders, in sort of a "If Rich People Can Do It, So Can You" bit of false advertising, and people are falling for it.

What do you get when you take this bait and set up a perpetual trust, with just a few thousand dollars?

The Trust Peddlers' suggested contribution is usually five thousand dollars. Remember, a trust is a separate taxpayer and bookkeeping entity, and factoring out taxes and expenses, after the first one hundred years you can expect this thing to grow to, say, sixty thousand dollars. That's right, all this gets you is the price of a decently equipped pickup truck, in *today's dollars*, in a hundred years. Congratulations:

You've now guaranteed that you've set something up that is an expensive pain in the ass to maintain. It's legally supposed to hang around until the cockroaches take over the planet, and right about then, it will really be worth something.

I've had people walk in who've set up a bunch of these things, and now that they need the dough for college tuition or retirement, they're desperate to bust them up. As a lawyer, I can't really advise them to disregard the law and take these mini-trusts out into the alley and burn the documents, so all I can do is suggest they go to court and try to get an order dissolving these little trusts, which in some states works and in some it doesn't.

There's other follies I've seen from people drunk on trusts, like setting up multiple trusts that frustrate, instead of foster, the client's purposes. Take the case of dueling trusts: When you sign a will, it typically has language that declares it to be your *Last* Will and Testament. That's not just flowery, say-you're-gonna-die language, it means something—the only will that counts is the last one you sign. Even if the last will doesn't say so, state laws tell the courts to disregard all your old wills and just probate the last thing you signed before checking out.

Well, there's no such rule for trusts: Each one you sign is a separate pocket of money that lives on forever, or until your trust document says to kill it. So, what if the trust is a substitute for your will, and what if you sign a bunch and they all say something different?

A Case Where the Right Hand Doesn't Know What the Left Hand is Doing

Bob was getting old and had saved a bunch of money, but he wasn't married and didn't have kids. He was close to his siblings, nieces and nephews, but he secretly wanted to set aside money for promoting one of his obsessions: Proving that the United States Space Program moon landings were all a hoax, filmed on a Hollywood backlot. He knew his relatives would think he was screwy for setting money aside in trust for the moon-landing thing, and he'd always given his bother Tom a copy of his old wills and trusts without provisions exposing "Moongate", since Tom was going to be the executor and trustee at Bob's death.

Torn between fulfilling his life's dream of finally exposing that faker Neil Armstrong, on the one hand, and disappointing his family on the other, Bob punted: He went to lawyer number one, and signed a will and a trust that set all his money aside for the fake-moon-landing project, secretly leaving those documents with lawyer number one, who was named to carry out the mission as successor trustee at Bob's death. Then, after a few months of hand wringing and guilt feelings, he broke down, changed his mind, and went to lawyer number two and did a completely different will and trust, leaving everything to his siblings and their kids. He gave *these* documents to brother Tom, without mentioning the moon-landing trust he thought he'd just killed.

When Bob died, brother Tom and lawyer number two, thinking they have the last word, moved to probate the will and set up the trust for the family members, when, Surprise! Out popped lawyer number one, who claimed everything in the name of the Fake Moon Landing Foundation, with the earlier-executed set of Bob's documents.

No problem, Bob's family figured, we've got the later will and trust, so we win, right?

Well, no.

Turns out Bob, with the advice of lawyer number one, *funded* that crackpot moon landing trust, by transferring most of his property into the trust while he was alive, a little detail he quickly forgot. Since there's no rule that says signing the later trust for Bob's family automatically knocks out the earlier trust for proving the moon rocks brought back are fakes, it appeared Bob's final wishes would be frustrated by simply setting up more than one trust for his post-death plan.

By now, if you've been paying attention, you know what happened: Lawyer number two sues lawyer number one to try to blow up the crackpot trust, and of course they chewed up half of Bob's dough fighting over this mess. Then, like most lawsuits, they settled, so nobody gets what they were supposed to get and the hoped-for public debunking of the space program, as well as Bob's family, both suffered as a consequence.

My point: Trusts—unless you're a zillionaire, you only need one.

11. INSURANCE: A DAY AT THE RACES

All insurance is a form of legalized gambling.

When you buy any kind of insurance, you're betting that something bad is going to happen to you, while the insurance company is betting the bad thing won't happen, or at least, it won't happen *when* you bet it's going to happen.

When you buy health insurance, you're betting you're going to get sick; the company is betting you won't. And, if you are reasonably young, you probably are wrong, you *won't* get sick.

Take casualty insurance, like auto or homeowners: You're betting you'll have a wreck or a fire; the insurance company is betting you won't. Again, if you're not a drunk or a pyromaniac, the company is betting correctly—they're taking your money for a fools' bet, but, *hey*, you're *scared*. And, anyway, even if you drive like you have an open bowl full of goldfish on the front seat, the state makes you buy that auto insurance, so some of the gambling is even state-sponsored.

At least, with health, auto and casualty, there's some logic to handicapping these bets, on both your part and the insurance company's: There's a reasonable chance nothing bad will happen and the company has better information about that than you do. You get to bet wrong, most of the time, and the company bets right, most of the time, or it would go broke. They make money, you sleep better at night, have a safety net if you get unlucky and bet correctly, and the government that ordinarily outlaws gambling everywhere but casinos, race tracks and church bingo parlors, looks the other way. Sometimes, the government encourages it. Sometimes they *require* it. Hence, legalized gambling.

I know, I know, you just came from your insurance broker's office and she had framed pictures of her kids posing at little league, holding those baseball bats and smiling for the cameras. She gave you a calendar and a key chain for Christmas, so she didn't *look* like a bookie. Well, sorry, but that's what she is.

Want further proof? Think about *Life Insurance*: Unlike casualty insurance, where there's a reasonable likelihood the bad stuff you're betting on won't actually happen, with life insurance, you're betting you're going to die, and the company is betting you won't, and of course, *you're gonna die* (See Chapter One). But people keep betting and the life insurance companies keep making oodles of money on this stuff.

How's *that* work?

Unlike casualty insurance, which is, at least, a socially responsible way of spreading the risk of dangerous activity we all need to manage, life insurance is *a product*. Selling it often goes hand-in-hand with death planning, but buying it is completely misunderstood and the decisions are emotion-driven. Like condo-timeshares in Costa Rica, you should not dive into the market unless you fully understand it. The best way to know what to do buying life insurance is to know what *not* to do.

Insurance works because the insurance companies are so much better at this betting game than you are. The companies have all sorts of information about you, based on *Demographics*, or population data that tells them how likely you are to die, get sick and most importantly, *when* you're going to do both. They know this from *Actuaries,* who tell insurance companies how long you're likely to live, when you will most likely get married or divorced or re-married, how many kids you'll probably have and when you're likely to get sick. Actuaries do this from pouring over mountains of statistics, which means you definitely want to invite a few of them to your next party.

When insurance companies price the risk of betting against you by issuing an insurance policy, they have the benefit of all this information; all you have, when you place your bet, is the same hunch you had when you cut off that driver in traffic today and sized him up, deciding how likely he was to shoot you. You're going on hunches; they're using data and computers. Not surprisingly, they usually win— they take your premium dollars and never have to pay out until they've made a profit off you.

Two things can screw up the market for this product: Not enough of those bad-betters buying the policies, and too many people successfully making claims. True, bad management can impact the *Solvency*, or the financial ability of an insurance company to pay out on claims, but they're heavily state regulated. Notwithstanding the conventional wisdom that much government regulation is pointless bureaucracy or a Commie plot, insurance regulation is surprisingly effective. Companies rarely fail due to mismanagement. No, their only serious problem is when the market for their product gets screwed up by an imbalance between those bad-betting policy holders to those winners with claims made and paid.

Since insurance companies *do* pay out on claims, *lots* of claims, their ability to meet claim payment obligations depends on lots more bad betters buying policies than those good betters, who actually do have something bad happen to them during the term of the policy. When the number of safe drivers no longer wildly outnumbers the bad ones, solvency is threatened. When this occurs, government usually steps in, on the theory that functional insurance prevents rioting in the streets. Government then messes with the market, by passing laws that prod or even force people to buy insurance, even if, instinctively, those people want to take a pass.

This is what happened when states started requiring mandatory insurance coverage for all licensed drivers: Premiums were getting expensive enough that drivers got smart and stopped betting: They stopped buying auto insurance. Auto insurers started getting into financial trouble and some went broke because there were too many folks making good bets and not purchasing, ("I won't have an accident, so I'll skip it."), and not enough bad bets, ("I keep paying these premiums, and get nothing in return."). So, government stepped in and said, "You want to drive? Go buy insurance."

Why am I dragging you through Insurance 101? These same market forces drive the life insurance industry, except there, the betting is even more irrational, since both sides know it's a sucker bet—the insured is going to die. A suspicious person could suggest that the only way to fix this is if the entire product is over-priced, since the insurance companies are betting against a deadly certain bad outcome (your death). They cover their losing bet by charging enough to be sure they make a profit anyway.

That alone wouldn't solve the entire losing bet that is life insurance, so you'd be justified in wondering how the insurance companies otherwise shuffle the cards to beat the odds on a bet they eventually *have* to lose. The answer: They mix up the market with lots of products. Nobody *has* to buy life insurance and the life insurance companies know the government isn't going to bail them out, so they scramble the betting by offering different, confusing rules of play. The games they're offering are called *Whole Life, Term* and *Universal Life*. Not surprisingly, they're all stacked in the companies' favor.

Whole Life means you pay and pay and pay, essentially for your *Whole Life*. The policy stays in effect from when you take it out until you die, and you're no longer making a sucker bet: Sometime during your life, you're going to die. This works for the insurance company because they're no longer betting that you're not going to die—they're just betting you'll pay them enough before you die that they'll make money on the deal. As usual, they're right: Whole Life is structured so that unless you beat the odds and die really young, the insurance company will be dollars ahead before you've paid in for the first dozen or so years under the policy.

So, why buy it? Good question: Typically, it's a bad idea unless you can't otherwise make yourself save the money you'd pay in premiums. Whole Life is essentially a forced-savings program, something that makes no sense unless you lack the discipline and staying power to save a few hundred or a few thousand bucks a year yourself. This logic doesn't change when you consider all the "Borrowing against the Policy" options, or dividend reinvestment and other policy claptrap designed to confuse you into believing the policies are a good deal. Those options are all designed to keep you from cancelling the policy by pulling out the accumulated cash value.

Once you've paid in enough premiums (usually, about year ten), the policy is a money maker for the company, even if you never pay in another dollar. Options like taking out those "loans" against your cash value, or "paying" additional premiums by "applying" your policy dividends, rather than paying out of pocket, are really designed so you forget the policy exists and leave it in force until your death. Just holding onto the money you already paid into the policy is a good deal for the companies.

Term Life insurance is the opposite of Whole Life: The policy only stays in effect for a term of years, usually five or ten, sometimes longer. So, here we're back to straight gambling: You bet you're going to die during the Term; the insurance company bets that you won't. The annual premium is a function of how young you are and how your health checked out—this is a straight mortality gamble, on both sides. Again, between the results of your physical exam (for a big enough policy, they'll make you take one) and their population statistics, the insurance company has better information than you do. So, don't buy this unless you really, really need the death benefit (More about this below). There's no investment in the policy, you're just paying the bookie because you think you'll die soon and your spouse and kids will collect the big payoff.

Universal Life is a hybrid of Whole Life and Term, with so many options and machinations that it requires constant monitoring and financial analysis throughout the life of the policy. It can be sold with a single, up-front premium, or with an adjustable or fixed rate premium over the life of the policy. It can accumulate cash value, but a lot of contingencies impact that cash value, like fluctuating interest rates. Unless you're a mathematician, I'd avoid these Universal Life policies, as they require you to become an armchair financial analyst and part-time actuary. One exception is using Single-Premium Universal Life to fund an Irrevocable Life Insurance Trust, but if you're up to your elbows in that kind of complex planning, you need a lawyer to help you sort it out. Don't try it yourself at home, as they say.

Now that you're an expert, we can address the question those moonlighting game-show hosts ask you on late-night television ads: "Why *don't* you own life insurance, when you can get it now, for just *pennies a day*, by calling this toll-free number....."

Once you know what you're buying, this is actually pretty simple. If you're a compulsive spender and can't hang onto a dime when it's lying around the house, consider a Whole Life policy in the smallest denomination they can sell you, usually no more than a twenty-five thousand death benefit. And, if you buy the policy, do two things:

First, pay the extra price for guaranteed insurability options. These policy gizmos are typically four or five opportunities to buy more insurance, at lower rates like you pay when you're healthy, even if you've just been diagnosed with something potentially deadly, say, Mad Cow Disease. They usually come up when you get married, have a kid or at specific ages you reach without dying. It's the one time they let you bet against the house and win. Exercise those options to buy more only if you're sick. Second, these policies accumulate a cash balance, based on the premiums you've paid over time. You can use this cash. As soon as you can cover the annual premiums by applying part of the cash value you've built up in the policy, do that too. Stop spending out-of-pocket money on the policy as soon as you can—usually ten years into the contract. There's no other reason to buy Whole Life, and nobody *needs* it.

There's also a time to consider buying a Term policy, usually a five-or-ten-year term.

Here's the checklist:

- If you're young, say, under fifty;
- If you're reasonably healthy, so your premium rating would not be sky-high;
- If you're working, making enough to support your lifestyle;
- If you don't have a bundle saved, meaning enough to support your lifestyle from investment income;
- If you don't have inherited money, and don't expect any soon; and
- If you have a spouse who doesn't work or your spouse works but couldn't earn enough to support your current lifestyle in the event of your untimely death.

If *all* these apply, then consider purchasing a large Term Life policy, in the neighborhood of several hundred thousand to a million dollars. If you're young and healthy, it's pretty cheap, because, after all, if you're young and healthy, it's a sucker bet you're making and the insurance company knows it. Try to buy coverage for a term that will remain in effect at least until your kids are out of the house and their college educations are paid off, when your living expenses will drop significantly.

Nobody else needs Life Insurance. If your insurance agent tells you otherwise, ignore her—she's just a bookie anyway.

Still, I can't be everywhere, all the time, just to save you from yourself, so:

An Eye for An Eye, A Tooth for A Tooth, Or Maybe Just One Hundred Grand for An Eye

So: A young guy, Mack, kind of a meatball, a junior, middling level executive who is pretty much desk-bound but otherwise has a macho complex, is enjoying a backyard touch football game when he takes a foot to the chest, seizes up on the grass and dies.

Widow, Michelle, comes in with his stuff and while they didn't have much saved, she's comforted to know she'll have some dough to pay bills because her husband Mack bought a bunch of small life insurance policies, which she drops on probate lawyer's desk like a fanned-out set of folded travel maps. *Over a dozen of these policies!* she cries, almost gleefully—enough to tide over Michelle and the kids until she can go back to work.

Problem is, as her attorney starts examining the policies, they aren't *exactly* life insurance: They're *parts* insurance, as in, *body parts* insurance. Whether dead meatball Mack was bamboozled by an insurance agent or just screwed up himself, what he's been sold are a bunch of casualty polices that pay you specific sums if you lose a body part: $100,000 for an eye; $250,000 for *both* eyes; $75,000 for a finger; $50,000 for a toe; $100,000 for a nose (A *nose?*); big money for an entire hand, foot, leg or arm.....You get the idea.

These policies are popular with models and movie stars, who insure their *eyelashes* for lots of dough. The catch, like all insurance, is that the companies *know* who's going to lose body parts but *not* get killed in the process, and desk-jockey, middling white-collar executives aren't those persons. These policies only make sense for people who work with moving machinery, like assembly line workers and farmers. Even then, the OSHA figures suggest there are only a handful (Sorry) of these accidents every day in the whole country, and virtually none occur at the office.

Michelle's lawyer applies for a benefit under all the policies, figuring, *Hey*, he lost *all* his eyes and toes, etcetera, etcetera, but the insurance company folks quickly point out that the fine print in the policies states you have to be *alive*, in order to make a claim.

"How could this happen?" surviving spouse Michelle cries out in cash-strapped anguish.

Turns out, Meatball Mack bought these policies in response to those phone-in ads on late night television, and the policies are all labeled "Life-Loss Disfigurement and Amputation Insurance," which apparently was *never* meant to mislead anybody, the "Life-Loss" part simply referring to the devastating *impact* on your life from having your nose ripped off your face.

Michelle's lawyer turns all the folks in the marketing and sales chain over to the State Regulators and gets a modest, but by no means full recovery settlement. As he tells Widow Michelle, "There's a reason that selling imaginary stuff, like insurance and securities, is regulated: You get ripped off when you don't know what you're buying."

Or, for that matter, when you're gambling against the pros.

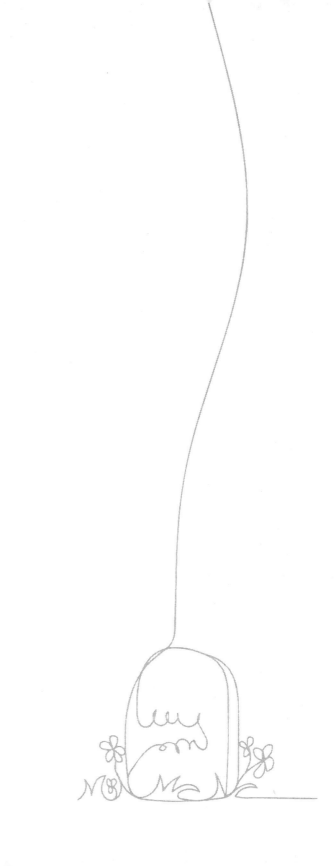

12. NOBODY LIKES A KILLER: SLAYER STATUTES BLOCK HEIRS FROM KILLING FOR MONEY

Remember O.J.?

For the people under the age of fifty who might be reading this book, Orenthal James Simpson, former NFL star and broadcasting celebrity, was charged in 1994 with the murder of his ex-spouse Nicole and her friend, Ron Goldman, a waiter in Los Angeles angling for something in the entertainment industry. It was a murder everybody but the jury thought O.J. committed (in the words of a Queens cab driver I encountered at the time, "I don't know who else would have murdered those people."). Simpson had a documented history of domestic violence directed at Nicole, and a fair amount of physical evidence linked him to the crime. And yet, he was acquitted of the crime, a result probably helped along by a mix of good lawyering and bad police work.

Not long after the criminal trial, which had been a media event, Simpson got sued again, this time with considerably less publicity. That lawsuit, a civil case, was a wrongful death suit by the victim's families, claiming that whatever happened in the criminal trial, O.J. still did it and owed the victim's families a bunch of money as a consequence. He lost that case and got wiped out financially. The wrongful death case was allowed to proceed for two reasons. First, since the victims' relatives were only looking to pick O.J.'s pocket, the second trial had no criminal consequence and therefore did not violate the so-called "Double Jeopardy" provisions of the U.S. Constitution. Second, the criminal acquittal did not have the effect of exonerating O.J. in the civil trial, because the standard of proof was lower in the Wrongful Death case. Essentially, you've gotta be really, *really* guilty to get the slammer or the chair, but only *mostly* guilty to be ordered to empty your pockets to the victims' families.

Wrongful Death just means, "I've got some connection to these dead folks and you're a bad guy who didn't have any justification for offing them, so give me your money." It has nothing to do with inheriting from those dead folks. Inheriting money from your victims adds a whole new element of *creepy* to the death business. Suppose that Nicole and O.J. were still married, she had money and that her will left it all to O.J., or that she had insurance payable to him, or even joint accounts with him. Take their divorce out of the equation (more about that later), that would mean O.J. stood to inherit money by reason of her death— something that raises the specter of people having impure thoughts, motivated by dreams of accelerating those inheritances by way of a little self-help.

Well, rest easy, people with scary relatives: Every state except New Hampshire has a so-called "Slayer Statute", the civil murder law that prevents people who "Intentionally, and without justification, cause the death of a person," from receiving any of that inherited loot.

Wait, you say—Why are we discussing this grizzly topic in a book about what to do when you finally get off your bum and go see a lawyer about your will?

Because, it seems that every black and white television melodrama from the fifties, with swelling cello and bassoon music and people chain smoking in darkened hallways, had some unfaithful spouse or spoiled adult child taking out a hefty insurance policy on somebody with the intent of offing that person and collecting the proceeds. The new stuff on cable seems to be rehashing that plot. If you think my outlook sounds dated, think about this: In forty years of handling probate cases, I've tried a dozen of these Slayer Statute cases. I'm a probate lawyer and I haven't tried a dozen contested guardianships, but spouses murdering spouses for money? Ring up the next case, Madame Clerk.

So, yes, it's still out there, bad people still haven't gotten the message, and I consider it a public service to clue in those of your friends, relatives and associates who might have designs on inheritance by baseball bat, to let them know it's time *to stop.*

Whatever side of this topic you find yourself on, be it scheming spouse or bereaved loved one looking to punish a murderer, you should know that the scope of the Slayer Statutes is so broad, there's really no way to get around them. Whatever the angle, the law has seen you coming.

Here's how Slayer Statutes work: There are lots of different ways somebody can get money because somebody else dies. You can:

- Inherit probate property, under a will or by intestacy;

- Succeed to a house or a bank account as a surviving joint tenant;

- Receive insurance or employee benefits by reason of a beneficiary designation;

- Become a beneficiary under a trust; and even

- Find some money in a coffee can under the dead person's kitchen sink.

While the details vary state-to-state, Slayer Statutes generally say that, regardless of what you stand to get or how you get it, if you, "Intentionally and without justification cause the death of the person," then you are treated for all purposes as though you died before the victim. The people who would otherwise get all the victim's stuff *if you'd never been born,* they get it instead of you. That includes the money in that coffee can—*everything.* The idea is to disincentivize people from killing people just to get money. Yes, plain old murder counts, but the killing doesn't have to be as purposeful as murder, just mostly on purpose, like you did something bad and it caused somebody to die, even if that wasn't exactly your main objective.

How's this differ from plain old murder? First and foremost, there doesn't need to be a criminal conviction or even a criminal case: Slayer Statute cases proceed independent of whether the cops and the State's Attorney catch up with the bad guys. Indeed, the cases are often used by frustrated families as a substitute for incarcerating the killer, when no prosecution is pursued because the State's Attorney believes there's insufficient evidence for a criminal conviction. Indeed, families often use these cases as an attempt to goad reluctant prosecutors into pursing what might be seen as a difficult murder prosecution, by showing that the wrongdoer is guiltier than he or she otherwise looks to the criminal authorities.

Second, it's a lot easier to nail somebody in a Slayer Statute case than in a criminal trial. I'm not just talking about the lower burden of proof. The bad act is different: "Intentionally and without justification causing a death" is not the same as "murder". The biggest difference is absence of *intent to kill.* Intent to kill means you're really *trying* to do the bad thing you did—it's not just a dangerous or aggressively stupid act—you got up in the morning and said, "I'm gonna *kill* my parents," and then, you did.

How's *intentionally causing death* different? Suppose you're an angry teenager, and your folks only let you use the car when you pay for your own gas. They check the mileage at night when you bring the car home, to see if they're getting hosed by your excessive driving. You're sick of the whole routine, so you decide to scare them as punishment by booby-trapping the garage door, so a bowling ball falls in front of the door if it's opened after you settle in for the night. Dad checks, your booby trap misfires and smacks him on the head, killing him. Don't count on any inheritance—while you may not have intended to kill him (that would be murder), you intentionally *caused* his death by consciously doing something that had his demise as a direct result of your intentional behavior. And, being ticked off at Dad for making you pay for your own gas is not a *justification* for causing his death.

And, since the objective of Slayer Statutes is to dis-incentivize killing for profit, most states follow an *indirect benefit* rule, meaning it won't matter if *you,* the bad intentional death-causer, actually get the money that pops up because of the death, or if some friend or relative of yours inherits the booty. That dropping bowling ball means nobody who makes you feel good about the inheritance can get an inheritance either, because that would indirectly benefit you. Remember, the idea is to not create any possible incentive for anybody killing anybody. There are cases all over the country where Slayer Statutes are employed to:

- Block the killer's minor children from getting the inheritance, because the killer "might accidentally, indirectly, benefit from the inheritance";

- Block the inheritance where the killer's ex-spouse would get the money as a result of the death because, "...Occasionally, ex-spouses give money to their former mates." (Really?); and,

- Knock out a resulting gift to a trust for the killer's *dog,* because, you guessed it, "A dog is man's best friend."

The Slayer Statutes are so broad in their reach they've been interpreted as the only way to override federal rules that require pension and profit-sharing plans to pass to spouses when married employees die. When a benefits lawyer showed me a court decision, ruling that a spouse would be dis-inherited from a pension when she offed her employee husband, I told her that result defeated the entire purpose of guaranteeing spouses inherit employee benefits, supposedly a major federal law policy.

She shrugged and said, "Nobody likes a killer."

In case you're not getting the message:

Playing Telephone When Murder's on the Line

Turns out there's this successful orthopedic surgeon, Bone Doctor, married for a long time to Very Nice Person, and they both look good in tennis outfits. They're living the good life, kids off to fancy, east-coast colleges, sporty cars in the three-car garage and Bone Doctor's practice is comfortably booming.

Mid-life crisis arrives and Bone Doctor gets himself a new, much younger Special Friend. She's willing to meet up with Bone Doctor at inconvenient times and do exciting things in hotels, but after a while, the Magic Fingers™ machine wired up to the hotel's vibrating bed loses its appeal. Special Friend starts pressuring Bone Doctor to do something about his spouse, Very Nice Person.

"Divorce is out of the question," Bone Doctor pleads with Special Friend. "We've been married going on thirty years, and she'd get half of everything, including my expanding practice, without which, our extra-curricular lifestyle goes out the window and instead of meeting at the Ritz, we're stuck in a Best Western out by the Interstate, trying to crowbar those tiny hooch bottles out of the mini-fridge without paying."

Meanwhile, Very Nice Person discovers the affair, changes the locks and files for divorce. With a little effort in divorce court, Very Nice succeeds in freezing their accounts, so Bone Doctor and Special Friend can no longer drain the accounts with overnighters at the Ritz. Special Friend is really angry: "Can't you do something?" she pleads with Bone Doctor. "She shouldn't be able to get away with this—it's your hard-earned money."

Bone Doctor, who like all mid-fifties-aged, mid-life-crisis males, labored under the delusion that Special Friend was just interested in his mature manliness, now senses that Special Friend would also like some of his dough and a bit of that Good Life lifestyle, both of which are threatened by Very Nice spouse's successful tactics. Worse yet, on the advice of their accountant, Bone Doctor had already transferred a bunch of money into Very Nice's bank accounts "for tax reasons," and their house, which represents a big chunk of their net worth, is in dreaded joint-tenancy.

"You'd be better off is she was *dead*," Special Friend, who's been around the block a few times, comments when she hears all this as Bone Doctor bemoans his legal predicament.

Bone Doctor sees an opportunity here. He can always find a new Special Friend; but starting over financially at fifty-four, after Very Nice cleans him out, *that* requires *work, real work,* and real work is a grind. Fine, maybe, at twenty-five, but now he's earned a break, and was hoping to live it up. The thing is, though, he's got to be careful not to do anything *himself*—with his hundred-dollar hair-cuts, creased woolen slacks and imported, calf-skin, tassel loafers, he correctly assumes he wouldn't last very long in prison. So the key is, encourage Special Friend to follow her instincts. She seems to have some pretty scuzzy hangers-on in her orbit—Bone Doctor wouldn't even begin to know where to look for that kind of help.

"Yeah, you're right," Bone Doctor says, mildly goading Special Friend on. "I work eighty hours a week for *decades*, and all Very Nice needs is a lawyer and all of a sudden it's all up for grabs. Problem is, she's healthy as a horse, all that tennis and no stress, so she's not checking out any time soon. And, with the boring folks she hangs around with, there's *no chance, and, I mean, No Chance* she's going to meet with any mayhem that would bring her to an untimely end. Looks like we're screwed."

Special Friend is no fool—she can take a hint—but like Bone Doctor, she's not getting her hands dirty, just in case this all turns out badly. She knows this guy, a car-parker at a club where she once worked, who always seemed to be able to get odd jobs done for people very discretely. She offers him some incentives to have a late-night encounter with Very Nice, as she's parking her car after her evening tennis match at the club. Car Parker Guy takes the dough but then decides life is too short. He splits it with his nephew, who's in the same line of work, and one night, when Very Nice gets home late, Car Parker Nephew strangles Very Nice to death in her back yard.

"A *tragedy*," Bone Doctor announces, as his lawyer moves to dismiss the divorce proceeding—can't divorce a dead person—but Bone Doctor's kids, who sided with Very Nice in the divorce, smell a rat. They return from fancy, east-coast colleges and go to the local cops, who suggest they get a lawyer.

As the investigation focuses on Bone Doctor, Special Friend and a host of secondary players, Bone Doctor turns on Special Friend, telling the Cops and anybody else who will listen, "Now that you ask, Special Friend *did* mention something about how much easier it would be for her to get some of our dough if Very Nice suddenly up and died," he says. "I never thought much about it, but, *gosh*, now that you mention it, you don't *suppose....?*"

While the criminal case focuses on Special Friend and her associates, the probate lawyer hired by the kids (Yes, by now you've figured out that the answer to all life's problems is to go hire a probate lawyer) tells them, "You know, the Slayer Statute can block Bone Doctor from getting any of Very Nice's dough, even if he isn't the one who killed her—even if he wasn't the one who hired the ones who eventually got her."

"How's that work?" the kids ask, incredulous.

"The statute says, "Intentionally and without justification *caused* her death..... That means, anything he did intentionally, anything that eventually caused her to die, blocks his inheritance. So, having an affair, creating the situation where his paramour, with or without his *express* encouragement, caused her death, should be enough...."

Sure enough, the kids' Slayer Statute case, combined with a Wrongful Death chaser, causes Bone Doctor to get knocked out of inheriting anything from Very Nice and her estate, including that joint tenancy residence, even though he's never even considered as the object of criminal prosecution. The cops can't even make the case stick against Special Friend—too many layers of responsibility down the chain-of-killer command. But, does Bone Doctor inherit any money off the dire deed? Not a chance, because *intentionally causing* somebody's death, when inheritance is involved, is the same as actually doing the dirty-work yourself.

Doesn't make any difference, because Nobody Likes a Killer.

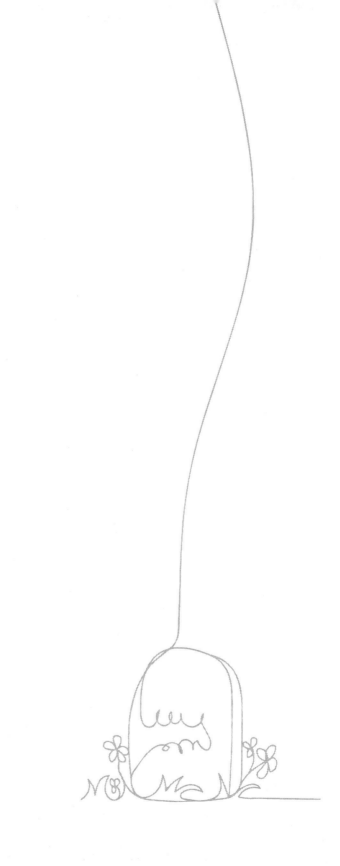

13. TILL DEATH DO US PART.....
BUT DON'T PUSH YOUR LUCK: HOW
DIVORCE IMPACTS YOUR ESTATE

And, while we're on the subject of modern romance, how about a few words concerning the impact of divorce on your estate plan?

If you think about it (and, apparently, most people don't), any divorce is going to have an impact on your plans for your property at death, so wouldn't you think folks would consult a probate lawyer before undergoing a divorce proceeding? Yes, this is a trick question, because almost nobody does, again, likely just to save a few bucks by not getting that second opinion. Just how bad is this bit of penny pinching?

Turns out, pretty bad. Know what the most common piece of estate litigation is? It's actually recovering assets ripped off from disabled adults, which doesn't make my case, so let's ask what's in second place? No, it's not will contests; not those nasty joint tenancy convenience suits (see Chapter Two); not trustee-bad-investment claims. The second most-common type of probate litigation is the lawsuit to enforce provisions of a divorce decree that obligate the dead guy to make payments post-death. Right behind that case in third place are divorces that challenge trusts set up during marriage, and lawsuits to fix that insurance policy or pension or I.R.A. that's still payable to your ex-spouse, because your divorce lawyer forgot to have you change the beneficiary designation as part of your divorce settlement.

One reason for this linkage between divorce and death planning is that divorce is the first time most people actually sit down and take stock of what they own, and it's a messy process. Quick: Without cheating by eyeballing the loose papers in your desk drawer, to whom are all of your cars, motorcycles and scooters registered? Who's the beneficiary on that term insurance policy that comes with your benefits package at work, that you probably never even knew you had? Who is the executor under that will you drafted yourself on the legal form you bought at the drug store? See what I mean?

Most divorces happen long before people are getting creaky-old, and without suffering through a divorce, old age is when people usually first get scared into going to see their lawyer. That's why divorce is often the first time you really take stock of your possessions, since you want to hang on to all of them and the divorce lawyers for your soon-to-be ex-spouse, want to take them all away. And, while I'd like to tell you the average divorce lawyer fastidiously hunts through your belongings and cleans up all the estate-related loose ends, my experience would suggest that statement is aggressively untrue.

In fairness to the divorce bar, let's face it: Most divorces occur prior to age fifty (The average age in America is thirty-two), and the number of people divorcing at an age where they're also thinking about dying (say, fifty and older) is just nine per thousand, not exactly an epidemic. And, for those people under fifty who are getting divorced, the split-ups occur because somebody is doing something self-destructive or abusive, or somebody wants to get into somebody else's pants. Under those circumstances, the beneficiary designation on that five-hundred dollar forced savings account at your credit union is not the first thing on anybody's mind when they sit, twitching through their first meeting with their divorce lawyer. It's: "How do I keep him from cleaning out all our bank accounts?" or, "How do I keep her from taking the kids to Uzbekistan with her new boyfriend?" Tinkering with work-related group insurance policy beneficiary designations is often the last thing on anybody's mind.

Many states have rules that in the event of divorce, automatically kill provisions for ex-spouses under your wills, even if you overlook them in your divorce settlement. Typically, those self-destructing provisions include:

- Gifts or bequests to the ex-spouse under a Will or Revocable Trust;

- Designations of the soon-to-be ex-spouse as Executor under your will or Trustee under your Revocable Trust; and

- •Designations of the ex-spouse to get your pension, profit-sharing plan or HR-10.

Not much of a list, is it?

Here's the stuff these statutes *don't* typically automatically cancel:

- Designations of your former spouse as your agent under a power of attorney;

- Designations of your former spouse as beneficiary under a life insurance policy;

- Designation of your former spouse as a joint tenant, on your house or on your bank account;

- Designation of your former spouse as beneficial owner of a land trust or power of direction holder under that land trust;

- Title documents that list your former spouse as the owner of your car, whether as joint tenant or just as the outright owner;

- Listing your former spouse as emergency contact with any school or employer; and

- Consents giving your former spouse access to your on-line accounts and social media networks.

There's more, but you get the idea—Lots of stuff is just not covered by those automatic divorce-blitzing rules.

So, here we go again: Yes, divorce is another one of those times when your first stop should be your probate lawyer, even if you're young and chipper, so you can't even *begin* to think about kicking the bucket.

Wait! You say. This book must be some kind of racket—this Guy's answer to everything is "Get a probate lawyer." True, I want you to do that when you get married, get divorced or before you get dead, but you go to the dentist every six months, the doctor once a year and nobody thinks that's overkill. And, there's a benefit to this sideways visit to your probate lawyer, pre-divorce, beyond simply not screwing up your divorce and leaving a mound of money sitting in your ex-spouse's lap that he could then share with his new Special Friend.

Doing the divorce right requires you to fill out a questionnaire and balance sheet, just like the one your probate lawyer should ask you to fill out when you first go to get a will and a trust. This is an annoying task you should gleefully embrace, for it will save you time and money in all future visits to the attorneys. You'd already have one if you did a Pre-Nup, since the disclosure forms on those documents require a balance sheet, but if you missed that boat, better late than never. As long as you're doing that, might as well be sitting with your probate lawyer and looking at your will, too.

And, if you live in a *Community Property* state (most of the West and Southwest of the U.S.), this will force you to take stock of your *Community* and *Separate Property*, so you have an idea of how much you'll automatically share with your spouse (the "*Community*") and how much you're free to give to anybody else ("*Separate Property*," which includes inheritances).

I know—you're still at, "Divorce is annoying enough, so who wants to bring another lawyer into the mix? How important can that be?"

Optional Divorce and Hundreds of New Friends

Chip, a computer programmer, leaves his job at an airline and moves to a new state to work at a Tech Start-Up, a place with great potential but not much cash to pay new employees. Chip's Spouse, Cindy, also a tech person, follows him to the new state and gets a different job, working in a shipping and packaging company.

Two years go by and Chip, seduced by the all the super-bright, edgy tech types at Tech Start-Up, slips into drug use, so Cindy files for divorce. They've both been well paid, so they've accumulated a lot of property during the marriage and their new home is in a Community Property state, so there's a lot of complication sorting out who gets what.

The divorce takes two years, but once it's over Chip stays at Tech Start-Up, while Cindy moves back to her old job in another state. Another couple of years pass and Cindy pretty much loses touch with her Ex Chip, who's still plugging away at the tech job.

Another year passes and Cindy gets a form notice in the mail—some kind of Securities and Exchange Commission flyer about some stock she supposedly owns, warning of penalties she'll face if she tries to "...sell, exchange, hypothecate, securitize or otherwise dispose of said securities...."

Cindy can't figure out what this is all about, but suspects it has something to do with her Ex, Chip and the Tech Start-Up where he still works, so with a few phone calls to the Personnel Department at Tech Start-Up and a couple to her divorce lawyer, she's figured out the mystery. Seems that when she got divorced, she and Chip both overlooked a truckload of then-worthless stock options issued to Chip when he started working at Tech Start-Up.

Stock Options are rights to buy a whole bunch of Tech Start-Up's stock at a discount, which become valuable when the stock price zooms over the option price. Since the options hadn't turned into money yet, at the time of the divorce nobody was really thinking about them as valuables. They weren't thinking about them at all, and their divorce lawyers never asked them for a thorough inventory— they were on divorce autopilot, using a bunch of canned forms, and in their world thirty-two-year old's didn't own a sizable chunk of the company where they work.

Turns out, Tech Start-Up is about to go public, selling millions of shares on the stock market at a price way over the option price. Options are compensation, just like salary and bonuses, so they should have been divided between Chip and Cindy in their divorce, years ago.

Cindy has her lawyer re-open the divorce proceeding, since the over-looked options are now super valuable. While the ex-couple is fighting over the division of the Options, another, bigger complication develops: All the employees and their spouses at Tech Start-Up are supposed to sign "Lock-Up" agreements. These contracts mean Chip and Cindy won't sell the oodles of stock they will get when they cash in their options. A big sale like that would kill the stock price and likely hurt Tech Start-Up and the public buyers of the newly issued shares in the initial public offering. Violations of Lock-Up agreements carry massive fines, so Cindy refuses to sign. After all, she figures, it's not even clear yet how much of the stock, if any, she's going to get. Chip is fighting the division of the option stock in the re-vitalized divorce proceeding.

Since Chip cannot certify with the securities regulators that he's the sole owner of the new shares of Tech Start-Up and Cindy won't sign anything, Tech Start-Up cannot get all its forms for the Securities and Exchange Commission timely filed, so they miss the window for the public offering. While the former spouses fight out the division of the stock issued from the overlooked options, the stock market turns bad. The falling market means that once Chip and Cindy get their option stock sorted out, the opportunity for other stockholders of Tech Start-Up to make a killing on *their* stock has passed.

All this because Chip and his now Ex Cindy and their divorce lawyers, overlooked a seemingly un-important asset when they handled the divorce. They would have been rich and would have needed big-shot lawyers to plan their mega-estates. Instead, they end up working stiffs, justifiably grumbling about the money they paid their lawyers.

You know the moral of this story by now: If they'd started out at their probate lawyer, the options would have been discovered in the planning process, and those options would have been front and center in the divorce. Riches to rags is a pretty high price to pay for squeezing out that second lawyer's bill, back when they first wandered into divorce court.

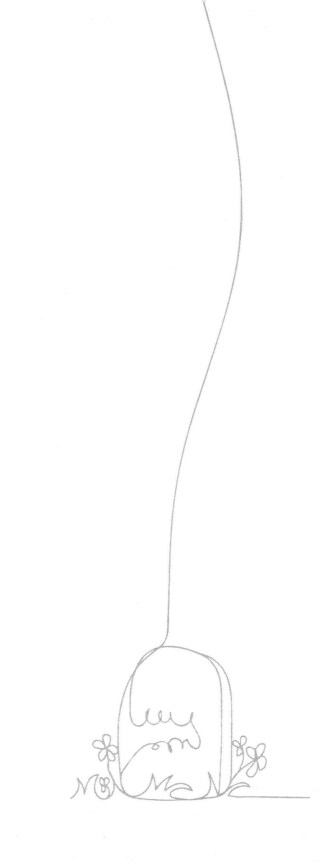

14. BABY MAKING: SURROGACY, ARTIFICIAL ANYTHING, DONOR ANYTHING AND TEST-TUBE ANYTHING

Time for another quiz:

What's the most important reason to make a will?

a. You bought my book, and it scared the stuffing out of you;

b. You're a Libertarian, so you hate that there's even a government in the first place, and you resent the state having anything to do with deciding who gets your stuff at your death;

c. You're a Commie-hater and love private property, so you recognize it's foolish to ignore making arrangements for your property when you die;

d. It's the only sensible, sane thing you can do for your spouse and kids, and the rest of your family; or

e. You're a male, so you don't really know who your intestate heirs *are*.

Yes, it's "(e)". You see where I'm going here: I'm sure there's one guy, somewhere in East McKeesport, Pennsylvania or Prineville, Oregon, who took his Catholic School Sex Education seriously, and prayed himself to sleep every night until he was thirty-two and then had sex with his spouse, for the first and only time in his life, then quickly died, faithful to her. For everybody else, there's "Surprise! I'm the child you never knew you had." How many men in America can say, with 100% certainty, that there's no possibility they had sex with somebody who then got pregnant, imagining the dreadful consequences of having your child and decided to go off and have that kid on her own? If you claim to be that guy, *you're lying*. Or, just as likely, you're fooling yourself—*you just don't know*.

The older you are, the more likely this is you: Before the 70's Supreme Court's *Roe v. Wade* decision legalizing abortion, people tended to have these babies. Then, there's *now*: Out-of-wedlock birth rates in the U.S. are approaching 50%. This statistic is a little misleading—the trend, up from 10% fifty years ago, has almost as much to do with married people having fewer kids and the decline of "shotgun weddings", as it does with the *ooops* phenomenon described above. Still, for most guys, while this might not be something, it's not nothing. It used to be that out-of-wedlock kids would have a difficult time proving paternity. The Supreme Court greenlighted heirship for these kids in 1976, and now, with advances in DNA technology, unless you, as the not-so-celibate dead guy, were cremated and there's no lingering trace of your DNA, proof isn't as tough anymore.

Wait, you say: Maybe you want your family to embrace anybody who walks into the courthouse at your death and announces their claim to your property for the first time? You want them to actually *give* the Surprise Heir a share of the pie? Really? That hasn't happened in any case I've seen in over forty years. I figure some combination of shame, uncertainty, indifference and shared suffering drives this rejection by your recognized family, because, unlike them, this Surprise! person didn't have to suffer through a lifetime of laughing at your jokes. That Fraternity of Misery compels most families to want to keep the pie split up only among the official, long-suffering survivors.

Having a will usually addresses this problem, by listing the people to be considered your family. Bingo, you've written out Surprise Heirs, which the law allows you to do. This certainty is one of the most important reasons to have a will, and yet another reason to shell out the fees for that will.

True, there are so-called, *Pretermitted Heir* rules that in many states can overcome the provisions of a will that spell out the members of your family. These statutes carve out a share for an out-of-wedlock child not named in the will, but they typically only operate for children born after the will is signed and when the omission can be shown to be purely an oversight—*Dead Guy just didn't know I existed, or he would have included me.* But, even the operation of these laws can be overridden with a will that lists your family members by name, or by a will that says, "My Children are Winkin, Blinken and Nodd, and I expressly make no provision for any other person who may be or may claim to be a child of mine".

With a properly-drafted will, you get to choose whether to include surprise children; without such a well-drafted will, your intestate heirship determination can dissolve into a litigated mess over un-anticipated heirship claims by kids you never knew you had, who make an intestate claim, with no will, or contest your so-so, not well-drafted will.

This used to be the only tough question your probate lawyer had to tackle in predicting your intestate heirship, which not only determines who gets what if you have no will, but also gives notice of your probate to people who get to file a *Will Contest,* challenging your will.

Not anymore.

You now have all sorts of new ways to reproduce yourself or otherwise acquire an heir and each of them creates exciting complications at death that you really ought to anticipate. Un-knotting them at death is expensive, uncertain and a screaming pain in the neck for all those involved.

Let's start with the most complicated, which is *Surrogacy*. In every state of the Union, in Puerto Rico, the U.S. Virgin Islands and Guam, and even in Russia and even *on the Moon*, it's illegal to purchase a baby. When you think about it, there's good reasons for this: It's a dangerous process, creates a black market for human flesh, encourages kidnapping, reeks of slavery and is just plain *creepy*. With *Surrogacy*, you have somebody who's not your spouse personally incubate a baby for you, get paid for the process and then turn the baby over to you at birth. That kid then becomes *your* baby. Since it's illegal to purchase a baby, there is one technicality: If you do this in a state where there's no law covering the process, you may be a criminal if you go ahead and do it anyway.

Fortunately, for gay couples and people who just can't successfully carry a pregnancy, there are such Surrogacy laws on the books, so a *Surrogate* can carry your baby, get paid for her time, trouble and the risks she's taking, then legally surrender the baby to you, to become your child. The thing is, though, *this is not legal in all fifty States*. And, where it's not legal, you are essentially buying a baby when you enter into a Surrogacy arrangement, so you can be criminally prosecuted *and* lose the baby. You can even get in trouble in a State where it is legal but you don't follow the rules. Other than that, what's the big deal? Of course, you're not asking that question, because, if you do this wrong, screw it up legally, it's a disaster.

Surrogacy laws require a written agreement that meets certain guidelines, and yes—sorry—you're crazy if you don't get a lawyer to advise you, regardless of what surrogacy agencies may tell you about just going lawyer-less and using their forms. Since the agencies charge a fee for "guiding" you through the process (essentially a legally-valid commission), some agencies often gently discourage you from having counsel. Ignore them, get a lawyer, and then, question one needs to be: "Is this legal in the state of the surrogate's residence?" The second question: "Is this legal in the state where we live?", although odds are the service you use wouldn't be operating in a no-surrogate state.

Why would a surrogacy agency ever steer you to a potential surrogate residing in a state where the process is actually or potentially criminal?

Supply and demand.

Surrogacy is rough on a woman—it has all the physical and psychological strains and risks of carrying your own baby, except then you have to give the child away. So, there are not a lot of folks who *can* do this and who want to do it, while there are lots of people who need it. This sends agencies roaming around the country, looking for anybody, anywhere, who might perform the service. In my experience, the agencies can get a little cavalier about where they find their surrogates.

You'll Need an Armed Police Escort If You Want to Keep That Baby

Tina and her husband would like to have a baby, but due to her maternal age she keeps miscarrying. Tina's doctor tells her that her only hope is to get a surrogate to carry that baby to term. Tina plans to go through test-tube baby conception, then have the baby carried by a surrogate. She seeks out an agency and finds the perfect surrogacy candidate—late twenties, already carried a baby of her own full term, with no complications or health problems associated with that pregnancy. And, she's thrilled to do this for Tina.

Turns out there's a lot of big words in that Surrogacy Agreement the agency has drawn up for Tina, so as an afterthought, she decides to get a lawyer to look at all the papers. The lawyer asks where the surrogate lives, and it's not Tina's home state, where surrogacy is legal, but a place Tina's never been. The lawyer looks at the laws where the surrogate lives, and she can't find any statute authorizing surrogacy. She calls a local lawyer in the surrogate's home town, and says, "Gee—looks like there's not a Surrogacy Law there."

"Yup," the local lawyer says.

"So, do they do this in your State?" Tina's lawyer asks.

"Technically, it's a crime here—essentially baby selling," says the local guy.

Pause the story here. Tina should probably have looked elsewhere, right? Wrong—she's *desperate*, like a lot of people going through this process.

"So, how do you get away with this?" Tina's lawyer asks.

"Don't quote me on this," says local attorney, "but our States' Attorney sort of looks the other way if the baby's for a heterosexual couple, but he'll prosecute everybody if it's for a gay couple."

Tina's lawyer was not crazy about the arrangement in the first place, but now she has a local lawyer telling her that they essentially only avoid criminal prosecution for going through with the surrogacy as long as the local authorities don't get politically backed into prosecuting all surrogate baby-makers equally. Well, Tina is forty and figures this is *it*.

"So," Tina's lawyer continues, "If we decide to go through with it, how does Tina end up with the baby? I mean, the agreement's not enforceable there, and the kid pops out of the surrogate at the hospital—don't those hospital folks *have* to give the kid to the birth mom or go to jail?"

Here's where it gets *really interesting*. "Yeah, in the beginning, I mean, at the hospital, sure. But, then, we have a little side agreement with the surrogate, where she and her husband (Swell—there's a *husband*) agree to put the kid up for adoption right away, and we have the biological parents go to court and adopt the kid."

"You need to *adopt* your own baby?" Tina's lawyer asks, incredulous.

"Yeah, usually it works fine—there's a lot of 'wink-wink, nudge-nudge' going on, but sometimes the surrogate has second thoughts and she tries to keep the child, and then it gets messy. We can usually get a court to enforce our little side contract...." Local lawyer pauses, like he's trying to decide what to say next, ".....but last time I did one of these, the surrogate and her husband weren't backin' down, so we needed an armed police escort, with a state copper riding shotgun behind the parents, drivin' 'em all the way to the state line, just so they could keep the baby."

Tina's lawyer is having none of this. She arranges to find a new surrogate in Tina's home state, rent them a place and have them reside there until that kid is safely in Tina's arms. Yes, it's expensive, but it seems like petty cash, compared to the costs and risks of the shotgun-escort-to-the-border adventure, described by the other Lawyer.

Still think it's a good idea to try this without a lawyer?

And, the problem doesn't stop with who gets to take the baby home. What about heirship and inheritance? The thing is: If you have a legally enforceable Surrogacy Agreement with everybody, including the surrogate, in a state that has a statute covering surrogacy, the baby is legally treated as the in-wedlock or otherwise legitimate child of the contracting *Intended Parents* for all purposes. So, along with avoiding the shotgun escort, that also makes the child the 100% legal heir of the *Intended Parents*.

What's the inheritance status of that child if the surrogacy deal isn't all legally fair and square? Well, just exactly whose heir *is* that kid? She was born of the surrogate, and if the surrogate is married, the law in all fifty states is that babies that pop out of married women are *presumed* to be the legitimate children of those birth mothers. That would make the kid the heir of the surrogate and her spouse, and *not* the heir of you or your spouse. Without a will, you'd better not go sky diving over the weekend, because if you should die intestate while your spouse is sorting out this mess, that kid is not your heir. Once you're dead, you can't even fix this with adoption—dead people can't adopt living people.

What if you live long enough to successfully adopt? That usually involves having a judge terminate the birth parents' rights, but who exactly *are* the birth parents? See where this is going?

So, get a lawyer and do surrogacy right in the first place, if surrogacy is the plan.

Baby-making heirship problem number two: What about those donor components, borrowing (or buying) other peoples' conception raw materials, eggs and sperm?

Ever since the first-timer, Loise Joy Brown, tumbled into the World in 1978, over eight million so-called "Test-Tube Babies" have been born through the process formally known as In-Vitro Fertilization, with over 60,000 in the U.S., each year. While many couples do this entirely with their own stuff, just using the process to address infertility unrelated to withering eggs and wobbly sperm, an unknown number of people use donor eggs, donor sperm, or both. What impact does that have on the parentage of the baby and its status as an heir of both parents? The reason I couch that as a question is that, with exceptions sprinkled around the Country, *nobody knows the answer.*

You're thinking, Did I hear that *right*?

Unlike surrogacy, which could be criminal if not legally sanctioned, there's often no law against donating eggs or sperm in a given state, so statutory regulation has not seemed like such a burning issue. As a consequence, there is generally less law and regulation on the subject. Again, whatever law there is differs, state-to-state. While much depends on whether you work through a sperm or egg bank, where the donors typically sign blanket waivers of parental rights and receive exoneration from any parental responsibilities, there are a lot of private arrangements by folks who may be a little suspicious about the quality and motives of those for-pay donors. With few exceptions, those relationships are governed by private contracts between the donors and the Intended Parents, or worse yet, by informal agreements or by nothing at all.

With potentially wild outcomes, like the baby belonging to two entirely different families, those contracts are extremely important, so, yes, sorry again, but don't do this without an attorney. And, the donors, too, should have an attorney, *and it should not be your attorney*. That's right—with donor egg and sperm deals, you need *two* lawyers, or the agreement may be easily challenged later, as in later-when-you-want-to-take-your-baby-home-with-you later. Private donors can get second thoughts and want some relationship with the kid you got used to thinking of as your child. Know anybody who likes *sharing* their kid with a non-parent? Yeah, me neither. The only way to be certain the child that emerges from a sperm or egg donor relationship is your child *and* your heir is to have an air-tight contract, which is enforceable under both the law where the child is born and the law where the donors reside.

Then, there's the entire Conception Derby arising from stored, frozen embryos. Many folks going through Assisted Reproductive Technology produce extra embryos that are frozen for potential future use. Since the usual contract governing this practice is provided by *the storage facility*, it fails to address what happens between the parents if an embryo is thawed later and implanted, especially in the event of divorce or death of one of the parents. The storage facility just cares about not getting sued if the embryos are used later or destroyed, so those contracts just address who signs the embryos out of deep freeze. They're not even *thinking* about whether those later-in-life popsicle children inherit from a dead biological parent. Again, get a lawyer; get a contract and change your will and trust to address all possible outcomes.

The bottom line: All the previously un-orthodox ways now available for baby-making, present issues which can seriously cloud both parental rights *and* the intestate heirship and will or trust beneficiary status of the resulting children. If you wander into this field without a lawyer to protect everybody involved, you may be creating more than one family with seriously fractured inheritance and custodial rights, and it will be *your fault*.

15. DEATH AND TAXES

My Italian grandmother, the one with all the bank account passbooks jostling around in her shopping bags (See Chapter One), believed that the only reason you needed a will was because without one, the State taxed your money and took it all away when you died.

I am always surprised to see that lots of folks still believe this to be true. There are now only five states with bona-fide inheritance taxes (taxes on you when you *get* an inheritance, which operate independent of the federal death tax); and another handful that have so-called "pick-up taxes" (state taxes that only apply, mostly if you have enough to owe federal death tax). Yet, everyday people are still looking over their shoulders for the looming death tax collector.

Some of this common-man death-tax paranoia is the result of successful political lobbying by the opponents of the Federal estate tax, who've struggled, somewhat successfully, to convince Joe Public that the estate tax is coming for them. I remember riding in a Chicago taxi years ago, when the Federal estate tax only hit people with five million or more, and the taxi driver rattled on about his irritation with the unfairness of the estate tax, when he learned I was a probate lawyer. "You have to pay a tax just *to die*," he said, repeating a sound bite from the anti-death tax lobbying effort. While it's possible cabbies are doing a lot better than I suspect, this person was probably safe from the looming confiscatory grip of the dreaded estate tax. More likely, this is evidence that people still have pretty outdated ideas about the relationship between death and taxes.

There's still a Federal estate tax, but it now only bites you if you're uber-rich, with an amount of over $11 million that you can pass tax-free to anybody, including pets. State taxes often have lower applicability thresholds, but it's usually millions, too.

And, *none* of these taxes, state or Federal, hit you *just because* you do or don't make a will, although without one, married people can pay some tax unnecessarily. Most of the time, if you're wealthy enough to pay the taxes, they'll apply regardless of whether you're intestate or have a sneaky, well-crafted will, specially designed to frustrate the tax collector. While it's true that these taxes can be minimized, deferred or even avoided with careful planning, those strategies only make sense if you're worth millions, or expect to get there by the time you die.

So, why do so many people sweat these taxes, people who will likely never see the death-tax collector?

In a word, *Folklore*.

There are some tax aspects of your will and death planning that everyday folks do need to keep watch over, so let's take a few moments to sort the tax reality from the folklore.

Some history—trust me, there's a reason you should know this:

While there'd been a few modest stamp taxes on inherited wealth before 1916, there'd never been a full-scale estate tax. World War I was really expensive, though, and in 1916 that was offered up as the reason for passing the Estate Tax, essentially the same tax as we know it today. It was then, and still is, a comprehensive wealth *transfer* tax on the value of everything you own and then give away at death, and while in 1916 it was touted as a shot in the arm to the War effort, that was nonsense. The Estate Tax has never been a significant contributor to the overall U.S. tax revenue base.

What was really going on in 1916 was financial panic—the U.S had been through three serious recessions in the last years of the 1800's, and had just suffered through a bona-fide depression in 1907 that was still being felt into the 1910's. There was fear and resentment about concentrated family wealth. The popular belief was that the impact of wealth concentration on financial markets was contributing to this economic volatility, with the populist backlash that ushered in the Sherman Anti-Trust Act in 1890 still hanging around in 1916. That populist spirit was the real political force behind the enactment of the Estate Tax.

Just as the Sherman Anti-Trust Act was supposed to break up concentrated wealth by busting up monopolies like the Rockefellers' Standard Oil Trust, the politicians sponsoring the Estate Tax believed the tax would serve the same purpose, by confiscating family wealth and forcing those rich kids to go out and get jobs like the rest of us. That empire-busting effect never really happened, even though, for a significant part of history (the 1940's through the mid –1970's), the top Federal estate tax bracket wealthy families paid was actually a whopping seventy per cent.

The estate tax never had this impact on the economy because the basic premise behind it was wrong: The U.S. has never generated its mega-fortunes primarily by massaging inherited wealth, generation to generation. There's lots of reasons for this, not the least of which being basic mathematics and geometry. Families multiply faster than wealth grows, so the inherited shares tend to get smaller and smaller, not bigger and bigger, in all but the wealthiest circumstances.

Sound like propaganda? OK, let's take another quiz:

How many of the richest 100 people on the Forbes 400 list of the wealthiest Americans, got there by harvesting inherited wealth and not through innovation and wealth creation out of whole cloth?

a. 100;

b. 66 2/3;

c. 52;

d. 21; or

e. 3

Right, it's 3, and I'm being generous there—these rating studies tend to over-estimate one-person's inherited wealth, by grouping together under one person's listing a bunch of family wealth parked in trusts and owned by siblings. Without that money scrunching, there'd be *none*. Giving the folks who compile this survey credit for this habit of impenetrable money smooshing, exactly three of the top 100 rich folks are primarily minding the family store, so to speak. The rest are innovators and hustlers who started out with a hundred bucks and contraptions operated out of a one-car garage. True, there's a healthy number of wealth tenders in the lower three hundred (although, still not the majority), but the big-players are mostly innovators.

The commonly-held belief that if you'd just wealth-tax the stuffing out of these rich people, you could solve all the economic problems in the U.S., was baloney then and it's baloney now. There just aren't enough of them (they're called *one-per-center's* for a reason), and those that do enjoy inherited mega-wealth don't die fast enough or often enough to make a huge difference in the U.S. tax base. I've crunched the numbers: Using the most liberal assumptions, if you zapped all the one-per-center's who die each year with a 70% tax on most of their wealth, you'd generate about half of one percent of the U.S. Government's annual budget each year. Nice walking around money, but not enough to implement the major social programs the advocates of these taxes worry about. While some argue that these sort of wealth taxes are a matter of fairness, (a debate for another book), they certainly don't do much to balance the federal budget. And, you *need* to tax *transfers* at death: Direct taxes on wealth are unconstitutional.

So, why am I taxing your tolerance for history and statistics with this tax lore?

The tug-of-war between the proponents of the Federal estate tax and its opponents, who constantly try to abolish it, results in compromises that continually move up the wealth threshold for picking people's pockets. That upward movement in the wealth tax threshold impacts just exactly who has to plan around the tax. It's an ever-shifting landscape, albeit moving in the direction of only taxing folks who probably need fancy planning and can afford it.

In the last forty-five years, the threshold for owing the Federal estate tax has gone from taxing people with only $60,000 (That's right—sixty thousand dollars—enough to tax-snare school teachers and paralegals who die with a life insurance policy and equity in a used car—talk about *empire busting*) to over $11,000,000—that's *eleven million*—today.

When the base amount was lower, everybody needed to factor in the impact of the Federal estate tax when drawing up a will. Today, not so much. True, there's talk of lowering this freebie, but still to multi-millions, not thousands.

I like to ask people this question, regardless of how much money they have: What would you want to do with your stuff if there was no such thing as taxes? This is the way all wills should start out, with a focus on what the lawyers call *Dispositives*, the who-gets-what-and-how-much part of the plan. Once that's mapped out, the next step is to decide if taxes will impact the plan, and then, whether to change things as a consequence.

When taxes do matter, it's because you have millions, and then you try to escape estate tax as long as you can. For most people who are married and have kids, this involves separating out an amount for the kids equal to the so-called *Unified Credit,* the free amount that escapes the federal estate tax, setting that up in one trust where your spouse will not have absolute control when you die. Then, you give the rest of your stuff to your spouse. This lets you tip-toe past the tax collector and then, even when your spouse dies, you only pay Federal estate tax if total family wealth exceeds two times the free amount, now *twenty-two million dollars* (state taxes can kick in at lower levels—again, typically millions). That's because your spouse also gets a separate but equal free amount and the trust you set up for the kids absorbed your free amount. So, unless both spouses together have over two times the amount you can give your kids tax free, you never pay estate tax.

When, over the last forty years, the free amount was under a million, and then, for a long time, just a million, that meant almost anybody with equity in their home and life insurance or pensions and IRA's, needed a tax-sensitive plan. That plan usually had two trusts, to make maximum use of the free amounts for both spouses.

Now that the *Unified Credit* is over eleven million dollars, an amount a tiny portion of 1% of the population actually is lucky enough to fret about, who still needs this sort of tax-sensitive planning?

- People worth over ten million; married couples worth over twenty million, and fewer millions if there's a state death tax;

- People who aren't at ten million yet, but expect to inherit money or come into a windfall that could put them over before they die;

- People who own family businesses, where the value at death can balloon beyond expectation based on nothing other than a few profitable quarters of operations;

- People with collectables like contemporary art, that tend to both have unexpected value as well as sudden increases in value; and

- People with hard to value assets, like claims in pending lawsuits or patents and copyrights, all of which can yield surprisingly high values when professionally appraised at death.

What's missing from this list? People who aren't near the *Unified Credit* threshold, but just worry a lot and *everybody else,* just in case Congress slashes the Unified Credit back down to $60,000. Slashing the Unified Credit is something politicians talk about a lot but rarely do—it hasn't gone *down* in value in the forty years I've been practicing law. This large-scale ability of most folks to ignore the estate tax is important when you get your will done: The two-trust, straight-jacket planning I just described, which is designed to defer or minimize the Federal estate tax, often generates a very different will and trust than you'd get just answering the question, What would you do if there's no taxes?

Setting up trusts you don't need or want, just because you *might* get nicked by the estate tax, is an expensive idea. You can use cumbersome formulas that automatically change your plan and sprout complicated trusts based on fluctuations in tax laws or values, but face it, the only move that makes sense—if you're lucky enough to strike it rich or unlucky enough to live through that first-ever reduction in the *Unified Credit*—is to go back to your lawyer for a new will. Those formula-driven, annoying trust-sprouting plans can surprise a lot of people, who were otherwise expecting to get your property outright. Now, instead, you have to live with the clanking machinery of complex, tax-driven multiple trusts—swell if they save you zillions in taxes, but clunky otherwise. Strike it rich, and then best to go back to the lawyer, *with your spouse in tow*, and start all over. With twenty-two million at your disposal, nobody will take out a collection for you to defray that nasty legal bill you'll incur, re-writing your wills and trusts.

And those state inheritance taxes? You can't really plan much to minimize those taxes if you're stuck in one of those states that still has an inheritance tax that operates even if you're under the Federal estate tax threshold. Those state taxes tend to operate at very low family net worth thresholds, and don't lend themselves to planning opportunities, unless you want to leave everything to charity, just to spite the tax collector. Better talk to your kids about that—my guess is they'll encourage you to try a different approach, like retiring to a state that's inheritance tax-free, which is now just about every state that's warm year-round, and no, that's not a coincidence.

If there's one thing I've learned planning for death over the last forty years, it's that there's a species of folks out there who hate, hate, hate the estate tax, like, deep down into their bone marrow—more than they hate income taxes, or state licensing taxes, or commercial-strip zoning, or disco music or airport terminals. The thinking goes something like this: I've spent my entire life accumulating wealth and building private property, and the things that make this a Great Country are the regard we have for private wealth and the lengths we go to preserving and protecting private property rights. So, this tax on *my wealth* is an affront to everything I hold dear and to the principles that make this country great, etcetera, etcetera.

Folks who think this way go to remarkable efforts to minimize, leverage or even eliminate the Federal estate tax, but the thing is, those efforts work much better if you're a zillionaire, than, say, you're just about at the Unified Credit, eleven million dollar free-amount threshold. That's because these tax-driven structures require you to give up a lot of control over the property placed in these trusts. Giving up that control over your property is less painful if you've got so much dough you can mostly do without whatever you parked in those trusts.

For everybody else, there's this:

I Know It's in One of Those Countries Out There

There's this Guy, call him "Tax Hater", he's been a regular customer of his tax lawyers over the years. A couple of decades ago, when the free amount, that Unified Credit against the estate tax was just one million, Tax Hater went to his lawyer and said, "What can I do so I never have to pay this darned death tax?"

Tax Hater didn't have a lot of options. He was in that netherworld between having just enough to be troubled by the tax, but not enough to fund complex leveraging devices with money he'd never need to touch again. His lawyer, a creative sort without my common-sense perspective, suggested setting up a foreign trust, one managed offshore with a foreign corporate trustee. Those gizmos were easier to set up in the 1990's, with fewer reporting and anti-fraud rules to work around. And, Tax Hater was told, the foreign trust would have creditor-protection superpowers, the ability to dodge bill collectors and other people suing Tax Hater, all in a single leap.

So, Tax Hater transferred most of his then liquid assets into a foreign trust, one where his kids would eventually get the income, but it otherwise was out of his orbit completely.

Now, twenty years later, he's seeing a new lawyer, because, Tax Hater claims, "He got mislead by that other Tax Lawyer Guy." Now that the Unified Credit is *11 million dollars,* way over his net worth, *including* the value of the dough he's got parked in that offshore trust, he wants his money back.

"You know," New Lawyer tells Tax Hater, "the reason these foreign trusts avoid the estate tax is you can't get the money back—you effectively gave it away when you set it up, all those years ago. Where'd you say the money was parked?"

"It's *Islands*, like, maybe 'Canary', or 'Cook', or—"

"*Cayman*?" New Lawyer suggests. "They do a lot of those out there."

Right—he doesn't even know *which* Country the money is stashed in.

"There's lots of new reporting rules with these Foreign Trusts these days. Are you sure you're in complete compliance?" New Lawyer askes.

Once New Lawyer gets ahold of trust statements, it's clear Tax Hater is wildly out of reporting compliance, and owes the Federal government a bunch of fees and penalties, which, even if he could get the money back (he can't), would wipe out much of the remaining value.

The only humane thing New Lawyer can do is to tell him the news, tell him to repent, send him on his way and hope he never returns.

This happens more than you'd expect—people doing extraordinary and inappropriate planning, only to satisfy a visceral hatred of the estate tax, then end up effectively shooting themselves in the tax foot, by losing control over the money, or access to it, or both.

The ultimate irony of the death and taxes aspect of this process is what's actually occurred as a consequence of Congress jacking up the *Unified Credit* to 11-plus million dollars. Remember my grandmother? The one who thought you needed a will to avoid having the government take all your property with taxes? Well, her ghost still haunts the death planning process. The unintended result of taking just about everybody out of the estate tax liability avoidance racket is that people have stopped going to estate and death planning lawyers in droves. The logic seems to be that before, when you were paying legal fees to avoid thousands in taxes, while you hated paying those darned lawyers, it was better than paying the !&$#@& Government. That motivation's gone, so now, apparently, legal fees are all that's cursed, and more and more people are accidentally dying without wills and leaving what they do have to distant relatives in East German prisons (See Chapter One).

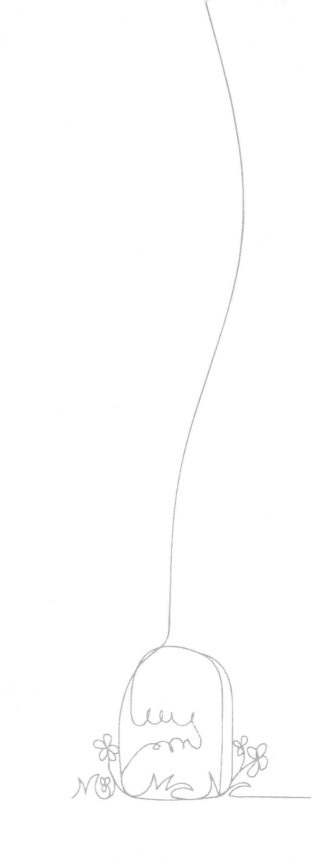

16. WILL CONTESTS AND OTHER FOOD FIGHTS

If you happen to still have young kids or grandkids, try this experiment:

Get into the front seat of your car, then have the kids slide into the back seat—this works best with three kids or more, particularly if you wedge them all into that back seat close together, so they get to squirm and rub shoulders. OK, now, once they stop yelling stuff like, "Stop looking at me! She's *looking* at me," pull something tasty out of your pocket and turn to face the crowd. Works best with a doughnut or a candy bar. "Does anybody want this?" you ask. Be sure to add, "I only have *one*," just in case somebody's not hungry. What happens? "Me! Me!" predictably, from everybody. "OK, I'll just break it up," you announce, as you rip it apart haphazardly, to give everybody a piece. As you start handing the pieces out, *then* what happens? "Her piece is bigger than mine!" "I got the crumbly piece!" Or, my favorite: "You always give *him* the biggest piece!"

The psychologists have a word for this phenomenon: *Envy*.

And, the little reptilian slice of the human brain that apparently generates and controls this thing, doesn't get better refined or atrophy away as your kids get older.

One of my jobs is to handle the probate litigation where I work, so people are always asking me: "What can I do to make sure there's no will contest or other fighting at my death?"

And generally, before we get into all the technical defense strategy stuff (more about that later), I start with this: "Don't leave everything to your paramour or fourth spouse, and what you do leave to the kids, leave in exactly equal shares, with all of the kids having equal control."

Of course, nobody does this, in part because of that other reptilian slice of the human brain called, "I know better than anybody else what to do with my stuff and who to put in control, and anyway, *I want what I want.*"

If you exclude the cases where caregivers and other unrelated parties mysteriously end up in the will getting lots of dough and control over the post-death proceedings, the most common cause of will and trust contests, which are pure and simple attacks on the testation choices you've made, is violating one or more of the Four Commandments, which are:

1. Thou shalt not give unequal monetary treatment to descendants in the same generation, followed closely by;

2. Thou shalt not place only one or two of several kids in control, followed closely by;

3. Thou shalt not give lots of money to step kids, caregivers, second spouses, third spouses, paramours....well, you get the idea; and, finally,

4. Thou shalt not place step-families or second and third spouses in control.

Right about now, you're thinking, "Didn't he just give us a load of grief in Chapter One about how important it was to have your own way with your stuff? How's that square with this preachy business about not giving property to whomever we want?"

That would be a fair question, as long as you're willing to have everybody go through the Probate Litigation Death March to carry out your final impulses. The thing is, I've never had anybody come into my office, sit down to dictate their will, and say, "Here's what I want: Everybody sues the stuffing out of everybody else, and the winner gets a chunk of my estate....." And, if you're going to violate the Four Commandments listed above, that's pretty much what you're likely to get. Giving equal shares to the folks who stand to inherit anyway, with equal control over dividing up and managing the pie, creates the best disincentive against probate litigation. There's essentially nothing for the contestants to gain by fighting.

If you can't trust all the kids with shared control, there's always the Bank. Most major banking companies have the power in your state to act as executor, and they know what they're doing. While the kids may not like having the Bank in control as executor, it's hard for your kids to convince a plaintiff's lawyer, looking to sue over handling of your estate, that the Bank is evil and favoring one of the kids over another. There are lots of reasons for this, but the big one is because that never happens. The Bank officers just aren't that exciting, and anyway, they know their jobs and understand their duties of impartiality. Sorry, all you folks hoping to save executor and trustee fees by naming kindly Uncle Homer as your fiduciary—the banks and trust companies always make better executors and trustees, compared to your friends and relatives. The Big Banks won't take the smaller estates, but there's a bank in your town that will.

All the other defensive mechanisms, like no-contest clauses, video-taped will executions, pre-execution competency exams and contractual restrictions on inheritance, all require some degree of litigation to enforce, with attendant costs, barrels of legal fees and risks of imperfect outcomes.

I know, nobody is going to give up choices and preferences, simply to avoid all risks of litigation. But, as you formulate your plan, you should keep in mind the risks of every choice you make. Each one of the Four Commandments you break increases the likelihood of some squabbling at your death, and those squabbles generate the possibility your plan will not be followed religiously.

While these contests often happen, will contests are not easy to win. Most settle, in large part because they are often groundlessly brought by people who are simply unhappy with the will they were handed. There are two ways to go after a will: Claim the dead person didn't have enough of his or her marbles to do the will; and claim he or she was subject to *Undue Influence*, a form of hypnotism that isn't what hardly anybody thinks it is.

With the mental capacity standard essentially just-better-than age-blasted drooling, any will prepared by a lawyer after consultation with a client, where the execution ceremony is supervised by the same lawyer, is likely to survive a mental capacity challenge.

That leaves *Undue Influence* as the most common and only likely basis for a successful will contest. Undue Influence is generally described as influence over the testator in making the will or trust that robs the testator of his or her free will, replacing it with the will of the undue influencer. This requires more than just gifts under the will that were instigated by the nagging of the alleged wrongdoer. It also requires more bad outcomes than just gifts and bequests under the will or trust that seem unfair or unjust.

Things that *aren't* Undue Influence:

- That second spouse, who keeps nagging the testator to make a change to an existing will, so the will cuts out testator's kids from a prior marriage, where the testator gave in and made the change, just to get nagging spouse off his back—or even if testator gave in just to make nagging spouse genuinely happy.

- That provision the testator makes to name oldest child sole executor and trustee, in control of everything at death, just because that child insists he's the oldest and therefore entitled, or where he claims the other children are unworthy.

- That new will, where Mom's cutting out one daughter, at the suggestion of her other daughter, who's taking advantage of Mom's anger over the other daughter's attempt to place Mom in a nursing home for her own good.

The problem with all these cases of *apparent* influence is that they're not *Undue*; the influence results in *choices*, however seemingly unfair or unjust, or simply in decisions to make changes many people would disagree with, since they seem unsound. In other words, bad, unfair or just plain annoying testation choices are still *choices*. For influence to be *Undue*, it needs to overwhelm and replace the free will of the person getting nagged or needled. The assumption most people make, that undue influence is that unfair, nagging suggestion that the testator's kids don't deserve the money because they don't really love old Dad, that assumption is just plain wrong.

You can cut out—*disinherit*—your kids, or your spouse, or your favorite charity that was given a bequest in your prior will, for *any reason*—it doesn't need to be a *good* reason. Those OK reasons include socially inappropriate feelings like hating your kid's new spouse, or just plain arbitrary reasons like hating that green sweater your kid always wears. Because you can leave your stuff to anybody for any reason, you can disinherit your kid because she was a lousy driver and it really annoyed you. You can even cut out that museum you once named for a big gift under your will, just because they started putting all those kitschy, pop-culture banners across the main entrance, advertising exhibit tie-ins to the movie sequel *Dinosaur Zombie II*. It doesn't need to be a *justifiable or fair* reason, and it's not *Undue Influence*, just because the change in the will is made for a *bad* reason.

I've probably defended as may undue influence will contests, seen cases handled by other lawyers and been approached by as many potential claimants as anybody, and know how many bona-fide undue influence cases I've seen in forty years?

One.

Paint the Windows Black and Call Out the Dogs, Dad's Movin' In

Elderly Dad, a refugee who escaped Europe on the heels of the Holocaust, has always had a will leaving everything in equal shares between sons, Marc and Sam.

Dad's starting to fail, and son Sam lives out of State, so he moves in with Marc and his spouse, who fix up their basement so Dad can have a room down there. After taking care of Dad for a couple of years, Marc starts to get resentful of Sam, who's still working and hasn't been around much to see Dad. Dad's saved up almost a million bucks, and it seems more and more unfair to Marc that he should be splitting it up evenly between his sons under his will.

Marc and his spouse start working Dad over, suggesting, then demanding, that he change his will to cut Sam out. "It's only fair, Dad, I mean, where *is* he? He almost never visits, and after all, *we're* the ones taking care of you and spending our hard-earned dough to keep you in pureed vegetables and denture cream."

"Remember," Dad reminds Marc, "It was Sam who hid us in his attic and then smuggled us out of Europe when the Nazi Pogroms started. He even saved *you* from the Stormtroopers, in case you forgot." Dad steadfastly refuses to change his will.

Marc is really angry now. "We 'gotta do something," he tells his spouse. They notice Dad is more and more feeble, has trouble getting around, is getting forgetful and now almost never leaves their basement apartment. So, they hatch a plan: What's the one thing that could get Dad to cut Sam out of his will?

First, one night they paint the outside of the basement windows black, so in the morning Dad can no longer see out. Then, over the next several weeks, they begin making noises outside those windows, late at night. First shouts, mostly in Dad's native language, then they adopt a few dogs from a shelter, and they dangle hamburger in front of the dogs to get them to bark wildly near those windows. Then, to round out the effect, they buy one of those hand-cranked sirens, which they wind up at night so it sounds like an air raid, or a prisoner-escaping siren at one of the death camps. Spouse makes sure Dad is awake to hear all this.

"Dad, the bad guys have come back into power, I know they said it could never happen again, but there you go, and they're looking for *you*. How'd they find you? "Sam must have told them, just to throw them off his trail, he turned you in. Can you believe it—*bark, bark, siren wail*—he sold you out. How could he do this, Dad, after all you've been through?"

After weeks of this, Dad's not sleeping, getting more and more hysterical, crying himself sick at night, but then the noises suddenly stop. Marc and spouse tell Dad they've successfully thrown the stormtroopers off the trail, but, *hey,* just like the old days, they had to bribe them, and it cost their entire life savings. Isn't it time you cut that betrayer Sam out of your will, so we'll have enough to keep bribing the stormtroopers? Otherwise, they're coming back for *you*, Dad.

They bring in a new will and a couple of neighbors to witness it, and a hysterical Dad signs it, cutting Sam out.

Yeah, *that* qualifies as *Undue Influence*, and the will contest challenging that fake-stormtrooper will, succeeds at Dad's death.

So, if will contests are so hard to pull off, why am I lecturing you on thinking about potential litigation when you finally go to that lawyer to draw up your wills?

Because, will contests are the only kind of probate litigation where you control the outcome when you walk into your lawyer's office to draw up your will. You can be virtually certain that you'll avoid one of these challenges if you opt for equal treatment among your heirs.

Fights over whether your executor is doing a good job, or is unfairly favoring one beneficiary over another, are out of your hands—remember, you're dead by the time those fights break out. And, just what does that fuzzy, ambiguous phrase in the will *mean?* Those are all common battles that you can't control. Violating the four Commandments by giving kids unequal treatment, is up to you, but then you need to decide if making lopsided gifts among your kids is really worth the fight.

If the cost of having it your way ends up being endless, expensive litigation, don't say I didn't warn you.

17. TERROR: NO-CONTEST CLAUSES AND OTHER WAYS OF PREVENTING WILL CONTESTS

Ignore me. Go ahead. We knew this was going to happen. Violate the Four Commandments: Give a bigger share to your favorite oldest child; leave the beloved vacation home solely to your youngest, then make sure, just to *guarantee* a will contest, that you name your fourth spouse, the one who was quietly putting all your bank accounts into joint tenancy anyway, you make her executor and trustee.

The good news is that there's redemption for sinners in this business. There are tools your lawyer can give you to help deflect or even neutralize the bratty will and trust contestants that threaten to tie up your estate in litigation for years, making their lawyers the *real* beneficiaries of your estate. While there are several such booby traps, which have varying degrees of success, the undisputed winner is the so-called "*In Terrorem* Clause," (Latin for "In Terror"—*Oooh*), or it's functional name, the *No-Contest Clause*.

No-contest clauses work like this: First, you make sure the future beneficiary you expect to challenge your plan gets a big enough piece or specific gift from the estate that he or she, or more importantly, *their lawyer*, will sweat the prospect of losing that gift as punishment for bringing a will contest. Then, you add words to your will (and any trust you're signing) that say anybody who does anything remotely like challenging the documents, or any specific provisions in them, or even helps somebody else do that dirty work, that person gets written out of the will. They forfeit their share or specific gift. Done right, the clause is lengthy and goes at the end of the will or trust, to point out that it applies to protect everything in your will. If a beneficiary challenges the validity of the entire document, claiming that you'd lost your marbles or got your arm twisted, or even claims a specific gift to somebody is bogus, then the challenger loses out, sometimes even whether or not the challenge succeeds.

These clauses are enforceable in 47 of the 50 states in the U.S. If you live in Florida or Indiana, the two states that *don't* enforce them, move. Vermont hasn't weighed in yet, so there, you're rolling the dice. Every place else, use one of these clauses in your estate plan and you win, while that cry-baby, will-contestant kid of yours, loses—or, more likely, never gets around to actually filing a will contest.

The trick behind no-contest clauses is to make sure your lawyer provides that the penalty of forfeiting a challenger's interest under the will applies to *anything,* any kind of contest or litigation your kids and their lawyers might use to defeat your wishes. Courts are supposed to read these clauses literally and narrowly, because the law "abhors a forfeiture," lawyer talk for, "Don't take the will-contestant beneficiary's money away unless you *have* to, because that's a really harsh remedy." The practical side of this is that the no-contest clause needs to *expressly* list all the stuff your litigious kids are not supposed to do—don't let your lawyer limit the no-contest clause language to just punishing will and trust contests. Challenges to who gets to run the estate or trust, fights over how the money gets invested or distributed—these should all be expressly outlawed in your no-contest clause.

And, most importantly, given developments over the last several years, there's a new kid on the block when it comes to disrupting your estate plan: The *Intentional Tort of Interference With Testamentary Expectancy*. Make sure the no-contest clause mentions that lawsuit by name. The majority of states now recognize this new means of challenging your post-death plans.

Any *Tort* is a wrongful action taken against a person—assault and battery are both torts, as are cutting off the wrong leg in an operation, or ramming into you with a car. It's the civil law harm, remedied with "Just-give-me-your-money", bad conduct that might otherwise, if intentional, be criminal. A "testamentary expectancy" is the inheritance you had every reason *to expect* to receive, because you were named in a will or trust to get a share of the dough. *Intentional Interference with Testamentary Expectancy* means somebody did a bad thing to keep you from getting that gift or inheritance.

This *tort* arises in cases that would otherwise give rise to typical will and trust contests. The tort punishes the bad behavior that supposedly brought about the bad will, with one important difference: The challenger, if successful, gets money damages *from* the wrongdoer personally, the person who they claim messed with you to subvert your true plan. This is quite different from the remedy when somebody wins a will or trust contest: What that winner gets there is a bigger or better slice of the estate or trust pie. The Court puts things back the way they were before the bad will or trust got signed. Nobody writes a personal check as punishment; your remedy, when you win a will contest, is you get your fair share of the estate.

With the Tort of Interference with Testamentary Expectancy, the will challenger directly attacks the *wrongdoer*: Evil Uncle Herbie, who defrauded your Dad into changing his will with lies and deception, or conniving fifth spouse Elaine, who plied old Dad with hooch and told him his kids were trying to kill him, then shoved a bunch of documents under his nose to have him cut those kids out. What the winning challenger to your plans gets from succeeding with this tort is *Damages*, paid by the wrongdoer, from his or her personal funds. You can see why this would be effective to coerce people into settling baseless complaints of undue influence or scrambled brains—if the alleged wrongdoers roll the dice and lose, they don't just get a smaller slice of the estate, they get nailed *personally,* by having to pay damages.

I'm drawing you this picture of wrongdoing because this tort, valid now in the majority of states, has become very, very popular with estate contestants and their lawyers. That's not because it's any easier to prove. The wrongdoing required is essentially the same as with a will contest—you need to show somebody's committing undue influence or taking advantage of a testator losing their marbles. This tort has become the will contestant's lawsuit-of-choice because it puts so much pressure on the folks who likely were the winners in the big-slice-of-the-estate-pie derby that was Mom's will. When the tort case is filed, the favored beneficiary can no longer sit by and watch the executor fight the will contest with the estate's money—they now have to personally defend their own conduct and pay for that defense with their own money, *unless your will says otherwise.*

This tort also puts pressure on the dead person's lawyer who drafted the will or trust, as they can also be sued as potential wrongdoers ("Dad's lawyer did this to me! He always hated me and liked brother Billy.") That strategy of suing the lawyers can be effective, as they often have an impact on how the case is handled: They're both important witnesses and are often involved in defending the claims. Now, facing this tort, they have to protect *themselves* from financial ruin.

The tie in of this tort of Intentional Interference with Testamentary Expectancy to no-contest clauses is this: If you want your no-contest clause to disinherit somebody who brings one of these

Intentional Tort cases, the no-contest clause has to *say so*. Literally, the no-contest clause in your will has to say, "If any beneficiary challenges this will, directly or indirectly by, among other things, filing a tort against any beneficiary, executor, lawyer or other person by reason of the will and its execution, that person shall receive nothing and be treated for all purposes as though they predeceased me." And, this type of "Every challenge *including* the kitchen sink" no-contest clause is probably not yet in your lawyer's standard bag of no-contest-clause tricks—recognition of this tort is relatively new in many states, so *ask your lawyer to mention it in your no-contest clause.*

One more thing about no-contest clauses: People struggle to decide how much money to leave the potential contestant, since the clauses are no good if you don't leave the person enough dough to make their potential forfeiture a litigation disincentive. That fretting is mis-guided. These cases are complicated, so nobody files will contests without a lawyer. The bequest to the possible contestant needs to be large enough to scare off the challenger's *lawyer.* If the lawyer takes the case and loses, and the client is cut out, that lawyer is going to get sued for malpractice, unless they've given the client the most air-tight, "Don't do it," cover-your-ass letter ever written. And, if they've done that, the person is less likely to sue, so the amount you give needs to be big enough to make a dent in the lawyer's pocket book or insurance coverage. Any amount that's not peanuts will likely work, unless the contestant is already loaded, and then chances are, so are you, so up the ante.

Other standard defense mechanisms include:

- Videotaping the will execution;
- Having a doctor examine you right before you sign; and
- Purchasing a release from potential litigious heirs before you die.

Videotaping is not all that expensive, but you and your lawyer need to rehearse over and over again before the shoot, so it comes off *perfectly*—no adlibbing. I once saw a proud executor bring in his deceased Dad's execution videotape to preview, and at the end of the video, Dad looked at the camera, and the lawyer asked, "Do you have anything else to say?" Dad then announced, "Yeah, just one more thing. I'm totally, legally blind, so I couldn't read any of these documents."

Assuming your videotaped will execution does not have any unhelpful spontaneity like that, it can be used by your lawyer to scare off potential contestants once you're dead, even if it's not admissible as evidence in a will contest, which is sometimes the case because videotapes are generally treated as hearsay of whatever discussion they recorded. Just make sure the will signer looks good—feeble appearing testators tend to undercut the value of the tape.

And, always, *always* avoid gassing off on the tape about the *reasons* you're cutting somebody out of the will. Remember, you don't *need* a reason, and getting into your reasons for cutting out your kid is essentially just gossip on tape. "I'm cutting Sonny out because of that affair he had with Little Junior's babysitter," or "I'm cutting Sonny out because of how he hosed my daughter-in-law in his divorce." These sorts of recorded comments just open the door to a will contest where Sonny spends a lot of time and money proving he *didn't* have that affair or bankrupt daughter-in-law in that divorce. A simple statement by you on the tape, describing the general plan so you can prove you know what you're signing, should be enough.

A doctors' pre-signing exam usually doesn't help much, unless it is conducted by a psychiatrist, typically a geriatric psychiatrist. That's because those are the docs who analyze if you've lost your marbles, as a mainstay of their practice. You may not like the idea of getting psycho-analyzed by one of these docs though, since most folks don't like being told they need a psychiatrist, let alone someone called *a geriatric psychiatrist*. Grin and bear it and sit for the Shrink's exam, as other doctors are not as well qualified to give opinions on capacity, which renders those opinions on a par with layman's observations. Your foot doctor's opinion about how many marbles you've still got isn't a whole lot more valuable than the opinion of the cab driver who brought you to your lawyer's office to sign that will. On the other hand, it's nearly impossible for a will contestant to argue you could barely make a decision about who should get your property at death, when a geriatric psychiatrist says you were *fine*.

If you can't tolerate a psychiatric exam, the lawyer supervising your will execution (yes, there should always be a lawyer there) can run you through a test known as the Mini-Mental-Status Exam. The MMSE is a straight-forward and non invasive evaluation, available online with both questions and a scoring grid designed to be administered by doctors and laymen alike. It's a 30-point test, and consists of tasks like counting backwards from 100 by sevens, repeating phrases and drawing objects and shapes presented by the examiner. You don't need to be a psychiatrist to administer or score it. While it may seem a little simplistic, the value lies in that simplicity. A judge or a jury can easily understand why a passing score means you are still pretty glued together and why a failing score means you're not.

Finally, there's a new craze, which consists of telling the kids about your death-plan details while you're still walking around, then offering to pay your kids for a release and agreement not to sue when you die. Yes, it is exactly what it sounds like: Bribing your kids not to file a will contest. If that bribery angle doesn't pretty much kill it for you, I'll add that I've never met a client who wanted to even *tell* the family what was coming, let alone haggle over the ransom a kid requires to not blow it up. Yeah, I think these things are gimmicks, although they are probably enforceable, if you've got the stamina to stand up to your family and breach your privacy while you're still alive. Still: "Yes, Johnnie, I always loved your sister Sally more than you, so I'm leaving her the good stuff, and she's getting lots more than you. Sign here, indicating your approval....."; you can see why these agreements aren't very popular.

Just how important are these defensive measures?

File A Will Contest, See The World

A really wealthy client, who we'll call Real Estate Guy, has a wide-ranging portfolio of property developments in 35 of the 50 states. It's all managed in regions, with one of his five kids holding the reins in each different region. As widespread and valuable as this real estate empire may be, when he comes to see his probate lawyer about wills and trusts, the lawyer observes that the business structure is not unlike that used by the shoeshine guy in the lobby of lawyer's office building.

"You understand," lawyer warns Real Estate Guy, "that what you've got here are a few hundred buildings that are each probate assets. That means your will would need to be probated in each state where you've got a building. That's not all—your actual rental and development operation is a sole proprietorship, as in you, personally *are* the business, just like Luigi the Hot Dog Guy who runs the sandwich cart across the street at the train station. You sure you don't want to dump all the buildings and the operation into some kind of business entity, like a corporation? At least then, when you die, you only probate the whole thing once, in one state?"

"This works for me," Real Estate Guy pushes back. "I got a kid working each part of the country, and they sort of think of the buildings in their region as 'theirs'. I don't want to upset that applecart."

Probate lawyer is not about to give up, having heard this sort of thing before. "What about a succession plan? When you die, management of the whole thing will be up for grabs. You expect the kids to just sort it out?"

"Got it all figured out," Real Estate Guy says, pulling a couple of sheets of paper, folded lengthwise, out of his jacket pocket. "This is a list of all the properties, by street address. You do a will, and you give each child the buildings in the region they manage—I got 'em all listed here. That way, they'll end up running their buildings and their regions, just like before....."

"Don't you at least want to add a no-contest clause to the will, just to discourage challenges by the kids? This is a pretty complicated structure, so just as a precaution—"

"Naww, not necessary," scoffs Real Estate Guy. "We got so much wealth here, nobody's got any reason to fight—they'll all be rich, they get to keep their day jobs, and anyway, litigation would dishonor my legacy. That will never happen."

Lawyer throws in the towel and does the will exactly as ordered. Each kid gets just under sixty separate buildings, bequeathed to that child outright, and the will is executed with a whole raft of witnesses and notarizations, since it will need to be probated in thirty-five separate states. That's a national penetration that rivals several fast-food franchises, but no matter, Real Estate Guy wants what he wants.

Of course, Real Estate Guy guessed wrong. As soon as he dies, the kids go on the warpath. They're unhappy about everything: Some wanted control of the entire caboodle, while others are upset they got "stuck" with just the buildings in their region, since the values fluctuate wildly from region to region. The bank that Real Estate Guy appointed as executor goes about filing the will and petitioning the will for probate, one state at a time,

As soon as the Bank files for probate in the state where Real Estate Guy lived, one kid files a will contest. The contest is *bunk*, as Real Estate Guy knew exactly what he was doing and nobody got a lopsided share of the estate. The case gets tossed out without a trial, and lawyer, thinking the worst is over, files for probate in state number two.

Here's the thing: When you own real estate, in your own name, in more than one state, you need to probate that real estate with separate court proceedings in each jurisdiction, and the process is essentially a "starting over", in that whatever you did to probate the will in that last state doesn't control the process in the next state.

So, yet a different kid files a will contest in *this* state number two. Lawyer and bank executor think they've got this one licked, but when they try to toss out this will contest the case is allowed to proceed, since the parties are different, and there was no complete trial in the last state.

Thinking they've got a working plan, lawyer and bank executor file for all the probates at once, assuming that will force simultaneous contests that hopefully can be disposed of all at the same time, with only one trial. Like clockwork, a different kid files a separate will contest in each of several states—everybody wants different buildings and a bigger share of the pie.

The litigation proceeds in five different states over eight years, and is only resolved when everybody gets fee-fatigue and a settlement is reached. Ironically, that settlement creates a company that looks a lot like the structure Lawyer tried to prod Real Estate Guy into setting up, prior to his death.

"You know," lawyer tells his partner, "All this could have been avoided with a one-paragraph *In Terrorem* clause in the will—I mean, they each got a bundle, and any threat of losing tens of millions would have scared the whole bunch of them."

"What'd Real Estate Guy say when you made that proposal?" lawyer's partner asks.

"Something about 'honor' and 'his legacy'."

That's the problem with planning to avoid these post-death controversies—you don't learn the hard way, because you only get to die once.

One more thing, and you're going to hate this: Remember the retired probate Judge from Chapter 5, who told me the only witness she cared about in a will contest was the drafting lawyer, who then supervised the will execution? Her argument was that doctors, including shrinks, couldn't really explain how the medical evidence weighed on a person's capacity to sign a will or even the ability to understand the gifts being made under the will or trust. She believed that all the videotapes in the world couldn't really get inside the testator's head. But that drafting lawyer, *he or she* could explain how the decisions were made and how they reflected the choices of the dead guy. And the lawyer, unlike the doctors, was due back in court the next day and the next day on other cases, so if she fibbed about anything, she'd ruin her reputation with the Judge. So, according to the judge who told me this, that lawyer was the most important witness required to defeat will contests.

If you buy the Judge's argument, there's only one way to protect yourself, and that's go to a lawyer to draft your plan, then pay the extra dough to have the lawyer supervise the will execution.

Do it right—you only die once.

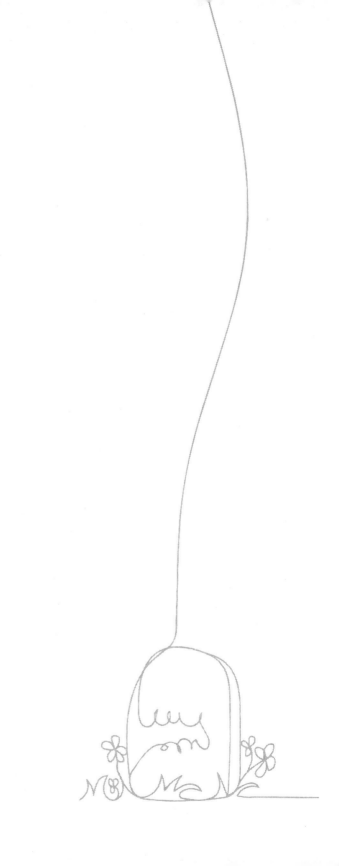

18. DOOMSDAY: WHAT YOUR WILL SHOULD SAY WHEN THE WORLD ENDS

Moving right along here, what are you gonna do if nearly everybody you know on the planet gets wiped out?

While you're mulling over the answer to that question, let's think about an equally disturbing, but much more likely scenario: Everybody related to you is at grandson Timmy's graduation at some far-flung college in rural New England, and the puddle jumper you all take home crashes. Everybody you'd expect to inherit, everybody you named to get stuff under your will, perishes on that plane.

Now, what?

The result here is *Intestacy*—remember *Intestacy?* That disgraced East German thug who got everything from the dead guy who never knew him, back in Chapter One? If you have a will, and everybody you name in it dies before you die, the result is your will doesn't do anything, and you're right back to *Intestacy*, thoughtless, brainless state law, most likely steering your stuff to some distant relative you've never met.

Unless.....unless your will has a Doomsday Clause, something your lawyer calls a *Gift-Over* clause.

A *Gift-Over* in your will or trust (It belongs in the trust if your will "pours into" the trust) is a clause that says, if all the folks you really want to get your stuff pre-decease you, then give your stuff to a so-called "default taker", sort of a back-stop gift so your will doesn't just hit a dead end, with nobody named. That's when you'd end up with *Intestacy,* essentially like you had no will at all.

The most common choices to plug into this *Gift-Over* clause are your siblings, or, if they're already dead, then the kids and grandkids of your siblings and your spouse's siblings. This is legally described as "One-half to the descendants of my mother, and one-half to the descendants of my spouse's mother...." Another popular choice is one or more of your favorite charities.

Two things: First, this is one of the most important, and, at the same time, the most overlooked aspect of your will; and second, it really shouldn't automatically go to those nieces, nephews and more remote relatives, which is often the brainless, after-thought choice— essentially the same result as intestacy.

If the entire reason you're doing a will is to exert some control over what happens to your stuff, having it fall right back into intestacy means you not only got that brainless, meaningless, makes-you-question-everything-you-ever-lived-for outcome of statutory disbursement of your stuff, but to add insult to injury, *you paid for it.* You went to a lawyer, spent good money for a will, planned everything out, and you ended up intestate anyway. Any competent lawyer understands this problem and is prepared to address it with a doomsday clause. So, why do so many wills lack one?

In a word: *Indecision.* People genuinely have trouble making up their minds about who to plug in as the backstop against *Intestacy* under their wills. I see this particularly in people without kids:

they hem and haw and struggle endlessly over what to do with their stuff. Those shirt-tail relatives seem undeserving, and giving it all to charity always seems like just *too much*.

Some folks solve this by inserting a doomsday clause giving everything to their Intestate heirs, which is kind of silly, since that's what happens anyway, if you have no doomsday clause. And simply picking "My intestate heirs at law" for your doomsday clause means you could end up with those kids and grandkids of your grandparents and great-grandparents, who are second and third cousins you've never met.

To illustrate how crazy that is, let's detour for a moment for a crash course about relations and relatives. People and popular media both badly butcher family relationships and mis-define them. Your first cousins are the children of your aunts and uncles—most everybody gets that right. Your first cousins' children are *not*, however, your second cousins—they are actually your *first cousins once removed*. Their kids are, in turn, your *first cousins twice removed*, and so on. People often refer incorrectly to these kids and grandkids of your first cousins as second and third cousins. In fact, your second cousins are the kids of your *grandparents'* siblings. Third cousins are kids of the siblings of your *great grandparents*, and so on.

The reason I'm bothering you with these trivia contest answers is: *Quick*, name one third cousin, a child of any of the brothers and sisters of your great-grandparents. I'll give you credit for a name on either your mom's or your dad's side. Right—you can't do it, almost nobody can, *so why are you possibly leaving them all of your money when you die?* Yet, that's what you're doing if your doomsday clause is "....to my heirs-at-law...", a thing you do only because, more often than not, you just can't make up your mind. So, you *punt*.

And, then there's charity: While I think naming preferred charities with a mission that you find sympathetic is a good thing, there are problems leaving the residue, or what's left of your estate, to charity. Doing that means that exactly how much the Save the Jellyfish Society ultimately gets is reduced by every nickel and dime your executor pays for anything, so you effectively turn that charity into a probate private detective. Charities are public trusts, meaning they have a duty to *everybody* to see that they get what's coming to them. Therefore, when you give them all or even a slice of your estate, they have to review everything your executor spent money on, even if it's innocuous, and they can drive your executor *nuts*. Worse yet, in most states, that gives the local Attorney General the right to look over the Executor's shoulder and nit-pick every dollar that's spent. And, if you split the residue of your doomsday clause between relatives and charity, it can also pit your relatives against the charity.

There's another problem with designating charity for a share under your will:

I Meant "Save the Seals".....No, I Meant "Easter Seals".....No, I Meant......

There's this vegetarian-environmentalist-socially-responsible-investment type, Aquarius, a former college professor, who's had a calling and is travelling the world, conducting environmental intervention to save endangered species. She's got a nest egg from years of teaching and modest inheritances from her parents, so after a brush with death in the Amazon, she's decided to see a lawyer.

When Aquarius lays out her plan to her Lawyer, she has this unfocused desire to benefit a large number of conservationist charities, so she wants to split the residue, or balance of her estate, among them. Lawyer asks for a list of the intended beneficiary organizations, so he can check them out, get proper, formal legal names for each, and be sure they qualify for income and estate tax charitable deductions. Lawyer explains to Aquarius the terrible cost of leaving money to non-qualifying charities and then having to pay taxes to boot.

"How much is that going to cost me?" Aquarius complains, dreading the cost of having her Lawyer fish through her list of intended charities with a magnifying glass, trudging through some phone-book sized directory.

"Not that much, but it's important," Lawyer pushes back. "Often, the popular names of some of these outfits aren't the names of the legal entities that receive bequests, and some of them aren't even legitimate charities."

Aquarius is not convinced, thinking this sounds like Lawyer-Fee-Grabbing Propaganda, so she insists on just giving Lawyer her own written list of save-the-seaweed-type organizations, and she tells her Lawyer to just write that list directly into her will.

After giving her fair warning, Lawyer does just that, and when Aquarius perishes in a pontoon aircraft accident in some remote jungle, Lawyer sits down to draw up the court papers for her probate estate. Those probate court forms require a list of every beneficiary named in the will, with mailing addresses for each organization so they can receive notices during the probate.

"You better look at this," Lawyer's paralegal warns, as she struggles to identify the 25 organizations listed in the will. Lawyer looks over her research and discovers that only five of the 25 "charities" named in the will are legally-proper designations of legitimate charitable organizations. The balance consists of a hodge-podge of well-intended, impenetrable, politically-correct-sounding, organizational word-smash-up. A few are informal names that could apply to more than one organization ("Wildlife Protection League", "Wilderness United Fund"); some appear to denote outfits that never existed ("Mollusk Protectors" and "Snail Life United"); and a few seem to relate to operations that are environmentally conscious but not really charities ("Bald Eagle Thrift Shop" and "Coral Reef Explorations").

Without a clearly defined list of beneficiaries, Aquarius's probate cannot proceed. Lawyer has to file a lawsuit to have the court do its best to declare which outfits are the actual, intended beneficiaries. Given the uncertainty, Lawyer has to name as defendants every charity that *could* come close to being one of those listed in the will, and since there's no way to give *every* charity in the book notice, Lawyer also names the Attorney General of his home state, who's charged with representing "....the inchoate interests of the People of the State of California, in seeing to the fulfillment of any charitable bequest....."

As a technical matter, I need to point out here that any will that requires the appointment of a government official to represent something called "Inchoate Interests" is a failure, right out of the box.

Anyway, this suit goes on for *years*, as the various organizations that could be in line for some of the booty intervene in the proceedings, until the list of parties is almost double the size of the original tally in the will. Ultimately, settlements are reached with three dozen organizations, who each get a share, just so the will can be probated and the beneficiaries can all get *something*.

This problem is even more complicated if the messy charitable designations are part of the residue, as the court doesn't even know who needs to approve legal and executor fees, expenses and other aspects of the probate.

A somewhat similar problem exists with religious organizations, because it is not always clear what *part* of the organization is legally entitled to receive bequests. Catholic parishes, for example, are not legal entities—that status belongs to the local Catholic Bishop of a given region. So, if you leave "your parish" money, while the Bishop may strive to expend the money on your home parish, it's really *his*, to do with as he sees fit.

Bottom line: You need to be careful with charitable bequests. Let your lawyer do the designation homework and try not to name splinter-sized, special-interest groups for the balance of your estate, opting instead for large, well-established, experienced organizations.

So, with all these legal potholes, how do you do a proper, thoughtful, effective Doomsday Clause?

Well, you're in luck. You've come to the right place. I'm prepared to tell you how to do the perfect, one-size-fits-all version of the Doomsday Clause.

Remember, the idea here is that your spouse, your kids, your grandkids—all the folks you'd normally leave your stuff to are dead. You want three things from a will: You want to have it your way, making sure your stuff goes where you want it; you want to help whomever is getting the money, so that the beneficiaries are *deserving* of what you're leaving them; and you want the gifts under your will not to spark controversy, or litigation, or the kinds of nightmares I've been pelting you with for the last forty-five thousand words. The Doomsday Clause should achieve all those things, in the event you have no immediate family survive you.

So, start by giving your stuff to people you *know*. Most everybody will have folks they know and care about, still hanging round. Assuming your will gets probated in some era other than the apocalypse, you're going to have friends and co-workers and people you've known for years that could really use the dough. Pick them. Your secretary, that person who's always cut your hair, that neighbor who's always looked after your place and picked up your mail when you're gone—leave them something substantial. Do it in fixed amounts, so they, like those pesky charities, can't gripe about how much the executor is getting paid, but give as many of them as you can a chunk of dough. And, make sure you state where they are living, *at the time you do the will*, in the Doomsday clause. Given the sticky nature of information these days, if somebody knows the beneficiary's name and place of residence on a given date, they can find that person even if they've moved away.

Next, everybody's got a cause or two they care about. If you live in a metro population center, there will be more than one charity that does almost anything a socially-responsible crusader can do. If you're in the sticks, there will be state-wide organizations that do everything. Again, pick organizations you know exist, and are settled enough they are likely to be around when you check out. And, like with your friends, give these charitable outfits specific, stated amounts, not the residue or a share of the residue. Then, all that pesky attorney general can do is make sure the lump of dough you promised to each charity has been fully paid. How much your lawyer charges, or how much that appraiser costs, are irrelevant to the charities and to the State Attorney General, if the charitable gift amounts are fixed.

Finally, let's tackle what to do with the balance of your property, or the residue. You need a mop-up beneficiary you are certain will be around unless the entire planet has been taken over by the cockroaches. And, you want one that gives you a sense of accomplishment and fulfillment from the gift. To make sure you see the logic of what I'm about to suggest, let's do another quiz (Sorry, I taught Grade School for a year and never recovered):

What is the one thing the average American spends the most on during his or her life?

a. Family

b. Education

c. Health Care

d. Transportation

e. Taxes; or

f. Location, Location, Location

It's "(f)". The average American spends the most on *where he or she lives*. I'm talking about housing, rent, real estate taxes, mortgage payments—all the costs that go into maintaining the place where you live. And, the reason for this is that the one thing we all do if we have enough money to choose, is we move to someplace we like to live.

Well, guess what? All those cities and towns and villages and counties—all of them are *Incorporated*, meaning they are legal entities which qualify to receive a gift under your will. They aren't just piles of dirt with roads running through, they are typically municipal corporations or subsidiary entities. They usually function surrounded by other entities, like school districts and park districts, that are all legally qualified to receive your bequests. And, they are *charities*, entities that qualify for tax deductible gifts

The best thing about them? *They're forever*. Your town, or your local library district or school district, will almost certainly be there, however bad your family's luck. So, make that Village you've always loved walking around in, or the public-school district that educated you for peanuts, or that park district that ran the park you jogged through every morning—make one, or a bunch of them, the residuary beneficiary at the tail end of your Doomsday Clause.

And, to make sure they don't just drop the money in their general piggy bank and pay a chunk of this year's personnel salaries, condition the gift on fulfillment of some mission you care about: The purchase of books and computers for the high school library; maintenance of that jogging path in the park; or college scholarships for needy students graduating from the high school. That way, the residue goes somewhere permanent, you achieve something important and you got to choose.

Your executor will have no trouble locating the village or park district where you lived, and the recipients so rarely get bequests they will fall all over themselves to make giving them money a cinch.

Little known fact: These Municipalities and their subdivisions, like Park and School Districts, are often exempt from the laws that give those nosy, State Attorney Generals the power to poke around in your probate estate after you die, another bonus.

Some will say this idea labels me as some kind of Commie or sponge brain, prone to whimsy-whamsy, and to that, I say, *Grow up*. Your local Park District is not a Communist Front Organization, and leaving it money so it can maintain that rink where your kids learned to ice skate does not make you Leon Trotsky.

I've drafted bunches of clauses like this, and even had a few actually operate well. You can die happy, and if you're lucky, somebody may hammer up a plaque with your name on it, so people will say nice things about you after you're gone.

19. GOD WILL DESIGNATE MY PROFIT-SHARING BENEFICIARY: EMPLOYEE BENEFITS AND IRA'S

By now, you've had lots of practice, so let's do another quiz:

What type of assets make up the largest portion of the average American's wealth?

a. Collectables, such as baseball cards, shellacked gingerbread houses and antique golf balls;

b. The equity in your cars, motor homes, boats and other vehicles

c. Insurance policies that accumulate value (This one's just to see if you've been paying attention)

d. The equity in your home

e. Employee benefits accumulated for you at work and other retirement accounts

f. Savings accounts, stocks, credit union accounts and other financial assets

g. Your pets and non-farm livestock

The answers, in order, from greatest asset to least: (d) Your home, (b) Cars and vehicles, (e) Employee-related benefits, (f) Savings, (a) Collectables, and (g) Pets (I'm joking about the pets).

If you picked (c), Privately-held Insurance policies, you get penalized and need to go back and re-read Chapter Eleven.

Home equity and vehicles leading the pack should surprise nobody; they're what most people own, if they own anything at all. That's why the 2008 Financial Crisis was so widespread—it involved home mortgages, vehicle loans and dropping home values, so it hit the average person hard.

What may be surprising is that employee benefits otherwise lead the pack, as the most valuable financial assets held by most Americans. And, to boot, they are the most widely-held financial assets among American households, too. For many people, they even outstrip houses and vehicles in value.

Employee benefits are the financial assets maintained by your employer, as well as private funds like certain tax-favored personal retirement accounts. These include pensions and profit-sharing plans, non-tax-qualified programs like salary continuation and forced-savings plans, group term insurance maintained by your employer for you, and IRA's (Individual Retirement Accounts) that you maintain for yourself at a bank or other financial institution. They often represent, for the average American household, the only financial asset component of family net worth.

The most recent average American household net worth figures are for 2011, and back then the total average value for these employee benefit assets was just under $69,000 per household. By contrast, the average total for household personal savings accounts was just over $5,000. So, it's not a big leap to assume that the biggest chunk of non-house and non-car savings for the average American is in those employee benefit and IRA accounts.

Why is this important in a guide to not screwing up your death planning?

Employee benefit accounts are the hidden treasure of estate planning, and I don't mean that in a good way. If there's a constant about these accounts and assets, it's that they are the one thing always left off those estate-plan-visit-to the-lawyer financial statements and overlooked when people talk about what they own. There are probably a number of reasons for this: People don't understand them and they're not in your face every day like your house or your bank account. People just don't realize employee benefits even need to be addressed in death planning.

These accounts are governed by separate contracts, so they don't just get roped in with everything else you own—they're not probate assets, like your cars or bank accounts, that simply fall into your probate estate and pass under your will. Instead, they require *Beneficiary Designations*, separate forms you fill out and leave with your employer, or for IRAs, leave with your bank, telling the employer or banker who should get this stuff when you die. Without those, the post-death outcome depends on default rules written into the original plan documents and there's no rhyme or reason to those. The outcome, without you signing a beneficiary designation, can only be described as the equivalent of giving a blindfolded monkey a fist-full of darts to throw at a dart board with names taped to it, then letting the monkey pick your beneficiaries by slinging those darts.

Why is that? Because the plans all differ, they're drafted by people largely unconcerned with who gets what when you die, and the plan terms *control* what happens if you don't designate a beneficiary. Some plans say your money goes to your spouse, if you have one; some say your kids, some say your estate, some even say to just keep your dough in the plan for a long, long time. You can't fix this problem unless your lawyer knows the accounts exist. Even then, you need to fill out special forms native to your employer, or special bank forms if there's a trustee in control who isn't your boss—the case with IRA's. If you don't use these magic forms, the people who run these accounts for your employer pick the beneficiaries—your desires and intentions don't count. These things are often overlooked. When that happens, nobody is coming to save you and guess who you might designate if you were paying attention.

I get it—I know these things are confusing, and when you call the personnel guy at your office about this stuff, he never calls back, then he sends you an email that is indecipherable and full of links to other stuff that's also indecipherable—I get it. So, if I can't scare you into running this stuff down with logic and common sense, let me try *shame*: If you don't focus on these plans and designate a beneficiary, you might as well burn some hundred-dollar bills off your back porch every night before you go to bed.

Why is that? That's pretty much what you're doing when you ignore these accounts. Un-attended employee benefit accounts are screw-up's on steroids, and the reason is *taxes*—not estate taxes, but *income taxes*. Those pensions and profit-sharing plans accumulating for you at work and those IRA accounts at the bank, are all *Tax Deferred*. That's lawyer talk for the government not getting its piece of the action when the money first got paid into your account by your employer, or by you with your IRA. Because these dollars go into your retirement accounts and IRA's income-tax free, they get taxed fully when they pay out to you, just like you're getting a paycheck. If that sounds vaguely un-American, keep in mind that the money was invested for years, earning interest and dividends while it sat there, and those earnings too, were untaxed. Pretty good deal, and Congress gave it to you as an un-spoken acknowledgment that Social Security might not be a real Ticket to Paradise, when you retire.

The reason ignoring employee benefits and IRA's is just like torching hundred-dollar bills is that if you're married and your spouse survives you (and, 99.9999% of spouses do survive the first to die), if you have a proper beneficiary designation, these plans can be *rolled over,* meaning paid directly into your spouse's IRA, and then you pay no income tax on that payout. True, when your spouse later dies, the money can't be rolled over anymore and if the kids get it, they pay tax when the checks roll out. But, there's another bonus: A good lawyer can jimmy up that beneficiary designation so the money rolls out to the kids real slowly, over a period of years, and it continues to be invested tax free while that's going on.

The numbers are remarkable: If you and your spouse die when those life-of-the-party actuaries predict you will, and your kids are twenty or thirty years younger than you are, this money can grow income-tax free for decades. If you start out at your death with $50,000, a fairly typical account size for a retiree, then your spouse outlives you by twelve years (again, fairly typical), after you die your spouse rolls your account into his or her IRA, your kids can then dribble out the money over about 16 years following your spouse's death. Do that, and that fifty grand is going to double over that time. Yep, another fifty grand, just for filling out the proper forms with your lawyer. And that's all money you'd lose without proper beneficiary designations, as none of this happens routinely under the baked-in plan default provisions written into your employer's plan documents or you IRA's. How many folks, when asked, "Here—sign this form and I'll give you fifty thousand bucks," would say, "Sorry, I'm busy, and anyway, I hate forms"? Can you smell those hundred-dollar bills burning?

But, losing out on the income tax savings isn't the half of it:

Support A Local Street Gang Near You

Bob, a dead person, has a POSWYLQ (It's pronounced "Posselcue", and is an acronym from the U.S. Census, for "Person of Opposite Sex with Whom You share Living Quarters"), named Sally. Sally comes to Lawyer's office with a problem.

"My Partner, Bob, had this Profit-Sharing Plan at his employer, Nuts & Bolts, Ltd. When I went to Nuts & Bolts to collect it, they asked for a beneficiary designation. They said they didn't have one on file. Bob never said anything about any designation and I've been through all his stuff and there's nothing in there."

Lawyer checks with Nuts & Bolts and confirms that Bob never filled out a beneficiary designation. As a long-time employee, turns out Bob has a three-hundred-thousand-dollar balance on account in the Profit-Sharing Plan.

"They gave me a copy of the Plan document," Lawyer tells POSWYLQ Sally. "Seems any undesignated balance goes to his kids if he's not married," Lawyer concludes, reading the Plan document. "Has Bob got any kids?"

"That's a problem," says Sally.

Seems Bob's only kid is an adult male, who's incarcerated in State prison.

"When's he get out?" Lawyer asks.

"Probably never," speculates Sally. "He's in this nasty street gang, the Insane Unknowns, and he solicited a couple of killings from the inside, once he got locked up."

The son's colorful pastime will not block Bob's street-gang-banger Kid from getting the Profit-Sharing Plan, since none of those murder solicitations were of Bob, who died of natural causes, choking on a hunk of sautéed baby octopus (more about that later). So, no Slayer Statute will fix this nightmare.

"Can Bob's kid even *get* the money while he's in prison?" asks POSWYLQ Sally.

"Not sure, but there are both profit-sharing plan and tax rules that say the money's got to come out, or they penalize you with a bunch of additional taxes," observes Lawyer.

Lawyer does what he can to try to change things, but nothing doing: The plan document controls, say the benefits folks at Nuts & Bolts. The staff at Nuts & Bolts take a bunch of forms to Bob's son there in prison. The payout all ends up in an account registered to Bob's son, who has in turn given signature power over the account to a few of the enforcers high up in the ranks of the Insane Unknowns, who will undoubtedly do something socially responsible with the money.

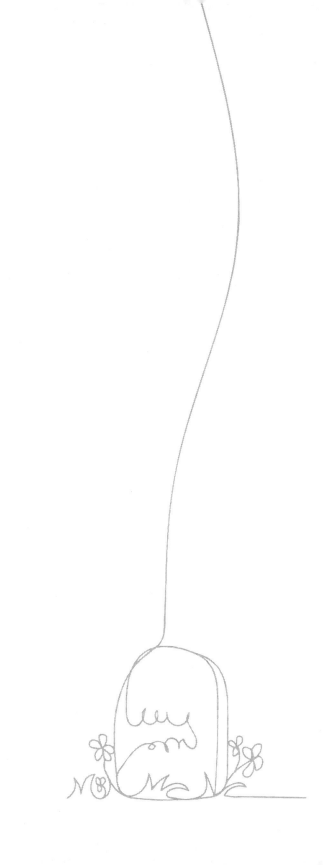

20. TRUST FUND BABIES AND MONEY AND CARETAKERS

If you've got school-aged kids, right now, you're probably worried about:

- Addiction to cell phones;

- Bullying at school;

- Are they gonna get *shot* at school;

- Drugs;

- Driving with open alcohol;

- That weird kid they just started dating;

- Slipping grades;

- Mononucleosis; and

- Getting into decent colleges,

Just to name a few.

If you've got enough money to be setting up a trust or a custody account for them, you're probably *not* thinking about whether it will fix any of these problems. What you should be thinking about is whether it will make any of them *worse*.

It's become a staple of estate planning advice to set up minors' accounts and so-called minors' exclusion trusts, on the belief that there's no better way to leverage against an eventual death tax than to start putting away the amount you can give a kid free of any tax bite (currently, up to $15,000 per year) as soon as they're born, and then repeat the gift annually. Swell idea, particularly if you're drowning in money, expect to die with over eleven million bucks and you can afford really fancy trust planning for the kid. Why fancy trust planning? Because, for this use-your-kids-for-tax-leveraging thing to work, the kids need to get the dough outright, free of trust, at the tender age of 21, when most of them are still drinking their way through College.

This is not like those silly, do-it-yourself perpetual trusts, where you only put in the seed money once—this is fifteen grand *a year*— thirty grand if you're married. Without any appreciation or income reinvestment in that trust fund, that's $315,000—over $700,000 if you're married—by the time the kid is twenty-one, so figure on the low side at least $350,000 to $400,000, available as the kid stumbles out of the bushes next to his dorm, fresh from some afterparty on the campus social calendar. Since most adults can agree that's not a prudent check to hand to a college senior, the way most folks deal with this is complicated trust planning, using so-called Clamshell trusts, which work to keep the money out of kid's hands, while using intricate and hard-to-manage notice rules. No such luck with the cheaper to administer custodial bank accounts, which just go *poof*, automatically, and distribute outright to Junior when the kid turns 21.

Some people really want tax leveraging like this, while some, who no longer need the tax benefit, just like the idea of accumulating a fund for the kids. Either way, I'll argue that these things are a bad idea. Nobody setting these up really believes having a minor's account with hundreds of thousands of dollars in it is a good thing—the entire enterprise is propped up on the practice of finding ways to actually keep the money out of human hands until the kid is *much, much older*, like, in most instances, thirties or forties or fifties older. That back-peddling requires elaborate record keeping and "encouraging" the kids to flip the money into new trusts that the kids are similarly "encouraged" to sign at twenty-one, unless you had one of those Clam-shell gizmos, and it worked—you sent out all the required notices and kept a record of them each year, etcetera, etcetera.

If you're a zillionaire, and can't go to sleep at night without knowing you've squeezed every drop of death-tax leverage the laws allow out of the estate tax, fine—go ahead and spend the significant amounts on your lawyers and accountants needed to do this right. For everybody else, *just stop it.*

Without the tax leverage, there's no reason to have these trust accounts around while you're still alive—you can continue to just pay the kids' expenses while they're under 21 or still in college, and even after that if you're paying medical of educational expenses—there's no gift or estate tax consequence.

Once you no longer have a legal obligation to support your kids, if they need more than $15,000 a year of extra help, you can *gift-split* with a spouse (pretend you each give half, wherever the money comes from—although, this requires filing a gift tax return) and give up to $30,000 a year, with no tax consequence, to each kid, or better yet, pay their expenses directly. If you need to give more and have it to give, you can go see your lawyer and spend some money using the trusts available for giving money to your adult kids.

Remember "Rosebud" in the movie "Citizen Kane"? If you're too young or just not an old movie buff, "Kane", considered by some crit-ics to be the greatest movie ever made, is the 1941 saga of an ordinary kid who grows up to be a fabulously wealthy and famous newspaper mogul. The character is loosely based on the life of real newspaper baron William Randolph Hearst. As Kane grows old and is consumed by wealth and fame, he dies searching for that shred of true meaning in life, calling for "Rosebud." Turns out the mysterious final, dying word he utters, that thing he's been searching for, Rosebud is *a sled*—that's right, a kids' snow sled, a $49.95 item at your local hardware store—that he cherished as his only real possession in his threadbare, childhood days. In the final scene of the movie, you learn that sled is Rosebud, as some handy-man mindlessly burns the thing up in an incinerator while Kane breathes his last breath, calling out for that sled that everybody else thinks is an old lover or a palatial estate from somewhere in his past.

The folks who made the movie could just as easily have been probate lawyers, because probate lawyers get to see, as much as anybody, the corrosive effects on young people of too much stuff. For most people, life is an endless process of managing and learning to live with *Scarcity*. In the typical, young-person's life, everything important is *scarce:* Time with parents; gifts from family and friends; and just plain free time, the liberty to pursue simply fooling around.

Growing up with money may have lots of benefits, but having too much access to stuff at too young an age can destroy a kid's sense that everything important in life *is scarce*. Dealing with scarcity and facing hardship develops character. The reason kid-Kane cherished that sled was not just because it was the only one he had, it was the only *thing* he had to keep him company, living in a snowy mining town with a couple of aww-shucks parents as his only companions. Shower a kid's upbringing with too much dough, or even let the kid know that *resources* are available and that ability to cherish relationships and things that are really, really important slowly corrodes, so long as the kid's outlook is, "Somebody will get me another one."

Corny as all this sounds, I've seen it first-hand. With Kid-Trust Funds around, at some point kids find out there are trust funds out there, waiting for them to dip in. Is it possible to raise kids surrounded by wealth without having them corrupted by the lack of scarcity and hardship? Sure, but with drugs and bullying at school and the other scourges of adolescence, why make things that much harder by having this money lying around, ready to spring out of trust at age 21?

I see more and more wealthy people spending big fees on a growing cottage industry of consultants, who advise parents on how *not* to raise Trust-Fund Kids, all with varying degrees of success. My advice: Save those consultant fees and just ditch the minor's accounts. Let the kids learn about their inheritance when you kick the bucket, at a will reading by your doddering old probate lawyer.

Need more?

Mostly Voluntary Re-Gifting

Doug comes begging his Lawyer for help: He's set up a bunch of custody accounts for his kid, Jared, and even set up one of those Clamshell Trusts, all to beat the tax collector by transferring money to Jared tax-free. Now, Jared is turning twenty-one, and he's kind of, sort of, not *completely* irresponsible, Doug says, he's only sort-of drunk most weekends, and he's only sort-of serially flunking out of college. Seems like now is not a good time to hit Jared with the almost half a million accumulated in these accounts. Lawyer notes that Doug has blown those complex notice rules on the Clamshell trust, so it too will also need to kick out to Jared, which means goodbye to all that dough. It's more than enough, say, to let Jared buy a motorcycle, throw a few parties, take up paint-ball warfare and engage in all sorts of other life-enhancing activities with the money.

"No problem," says Doug's Lawyer. Lawyer creates a new trust, one designed to hold all this dough until Jared is fifty-five, then he brings Jared in to *discuss* the circumstances under which it would be mindful of Jared to transfer everything he's about to receive into this new trust, *completely voluntarily*. A few suggestions are made, such

as the possibility Doug might otherwise cut Jared out of his will—
"Lots more where that trust money came from, sonny-boy Jared."
When that does not completely convince Jared of the wisdom of
taking what's about to be his and placing it in the locked-up-to-age-
fifty-five trust, Doug hints that he may have to use some of Jared's
unorthodox behavior to put Jared into big-person guardianship, using
one of those *Idleness and Debauchery* clauses in the state guardianship code (Yeah, they still have stuff like that).

Jared reluctantly signs the age-fifty-five-lock-up trust document, setting up that straight-jacket trust, and then Jared transfers
his newly-acquired almost $500,000 into that trust.

A few years go by and Jared, now a more mature adult, develops a mind of his own and he starts thinking about the events of that
new-trust-signing day, when it seems he might not have had his wits
about him, not to mention his own lawyer, to advise him of the soundness of the new plan.

Jared hires his own lawyer and they proceed to sue Doug, Doug's
Lawyer, Doug's Lawyer's Paralegal, who worked on that Age-Fifty-
Five-Lock-Up Trust, Doug's Lawyer's Secretary, who witnessed it,
Jared's Mom, who was in on the whole thing, and for good measure,
the limo driver that Doug hired to pick Jared up and drive him to
Lawyer's office, that fateful day. Claims of duress, legal gun-at-the-
head stuff, as well as fraud, undue influence and, for good measure,
one of those Intentional Interference with Testamentary Expectancy
tort claims are thrown in, a virtual guarantee the litigation will go on
for years.

Doug gets a new lawyer, who suggests they just bust the Age-Fif-
ty-Five Hold-Up Trust and give the money to Jared, motorcycles,
paintball wars and all. Unfortunately, Jared is in the grip of aggressive
lawyers and they want *damages*, so the whole thing drags on and on.
Jared never speaks to Doug again.

"You know," new Lawyer tells Doug, "All this would ever have saved you was a couple hundred thousand dollars in taxes, and then only upon your death, and *then*, only if you'd accumulated millions more than you have right now. Probably would have been better off never setting these minor's accounts up in the first place."

Now, even if I've spoiled your appetite for setting up trusts for your kids, you folks with minor children still need to see your probate lawyer about *Guardianship Designation*.

Even if you think you're too young to care about planning for your untimely demise, every state allows you to make a guardianship designation in your will, a statement of who you choose to act as legal guardian for your kids when you're gone. Not just the money person, but more importantly, a guardian of the kid's person, the agent who decides the care and custody arrangements, enrolls the kid in school and consents to medical treatment. Your will can tell the world (especially the court that appoints guardians) who you want to act as that guardian.

This is a relatively uncomplicated matter, as long as you are happily married to the other parent of your kids and you and your spouse designate the same person to act as guardian in each of your wills. The effect of those joint designations is that the court, which appoints guardians for your kids when you're both gone and they are under 18, takes your wills as *prima facia evidence* of your intentions. That's lawyer talk for, "This is who the parents really, really wanted as guardians, so we're only going to second guess them if there's evidence these are *bad people* who would somehow hurt the kids." The practical effect is that the court appoints the person you want to act, who will take custody of your kids when you and your spouse are gone, and then raise the kids to adulthood.

Some states even provide for such designations in documents effective before you die, allowing you to designate so-called Standby

Guardians for kid-care and custody during life-time disabilities, an outgrowth of the AIDS crisis.

Sounds important, and it is—well worth the trip to the lawyer, even if you don't think You're Gonna Die (See Chapter One). It also sounds too good to be true, and under certain circumstances, it is. Things get complicated if you're divorced, a single parent, somebody in a "Non-Traditional Relationship" (See the next Chapter), or just about anything other than a happy, married couple.

I'm always surprised by the intensity of the push-back I get when I tell clients these designations aren't like naming the executor under your will, who automatically gets appointed unless he or she is a convicted felon. In most states, these Guardianship Designations are *not binding* on the courts—they are just *evidence* of what you wanted. So, if there are conflicting designations of different people by each of the parents, which is typical post-divorce, or negative designations, ("Appoint *anybody* but dirt-bag, former spouse"), there's going to be an actual trial to determine who gets appointed guardian. The same is true if your guardianship designations draw relatives like grand-parents into court to fight the designations, like designating that same-sex partner from your relationship Grandpa always thought was vaguely un-American. In each of these cases, the value of the designation diminishes, since it is not necessarily going to prevail. The Court will always take your designation under consideration, but may appoint somebody else.

The best example of the possible trumping of your pick is that ex-spouse of yours. You may hate, hate, hate the guy; he may have left you for some near-teenager who spends his money like a bookie and you may have been conditioning your kid to hate the guy too, if you were the primary custodial parent. Your guardianship designation in your will may say, "Anybody but *him*." Too bad—unless he's an unfit parent who's had his parental rights terminated, your ex-spouse is going to take over as the kid's custodial parent. The fact that you were the primary custodial parent and designated your new partner or a grandparent to act as the kid's guardian in your will is almost meaningless. That's because your kids aren't chattels, in other words, property you can effectively bequeath to your new partner. All contested minors' guardianship appointments require a hearing on what's good for the kid, and your designation in your will is just evidence—important evidence, but just a statement of your preference.

Clients *hate* hearing this, and usually leave in denial, annoyed at this dose of reality. Don't shoot me—I'm just trying to save you some money so you don't spend hours driving your lawyer nuts, asking for all sorts of guarantees you can't get. Why *can't* you get exactly what you want, want, want, regarding who does and who doesn't care for your kids when you die? Because, as far as the courts are concerned, your kids are more important than *you* are, so they apply a *Best Interests of the Child* standard in deciding whether to implement that Guardianship Designation you made. If the choice rubs the court the wrong way, they're going to veto your pick and appoint as guardian that nasty ex-spouse, or that crotchety old Grandma that never accepted your same-sex relationship. Yes, and that appointee will have the right to raise that minor child you left behind, who, as a consequence, will not get a steady diet of the sensitive, New-Age upbringing you were hoping the kid would be fed daily by your carefully-selected guardians. Sorry. I don't make the rules.

This is often the most frustrating advice lawyers give clients, but if anything, the trends are moving away from court enforcement of your guardianship designations to defeat a Best Interests of the Child hearing. So, what's your best defense? *Don't Die*, the advice I give all my clients with young kids. You have more control over this than you think. While generally, another topic for another book, in the stupid-way-to-die-sweepstakes, I've seen it all: You fly around *in helicopters*? *Really*? Motorcycles? Enjoy snow skiing without a helmet? Date people you've met on the internet? Eat sautéed baby octopus? (As an aside here, I knew this guy who almost died, choking on a particularly gnarly piece of baby octopus. If there's any less appetizing phrase in the English language than *tentacles*, it's gotta be *baby tentacles*). You're Gonna Die—so take your time.

21. "WHAT BOX DO I CHECK?" NON-TRADITIONAL RELATIONSHIPS

Think about this:

One day, your third grader brings a classmate home for lunch. The kid's a little scraggly and scrawny, but you don't think much of it, since all eight-year old's sort of look like that. Nice kid, seems courteous, wolfs down lunch like he hasn't eaten in weeks and off they go to destroy something in your backyard. Over the next several weeks, he shows up more and more often, has lunch and now dinner with you regularly After a while you notice he's taking *clothes* home, clothes that he finds lying around the mess in your kids' rooms.

You do a little checking around and learn the kid is living with a grandparent; his mother is in and out of some kind of rehab, and nobody knows where the father disappeared. You ask the grandmother if he can take a trip with you, she seems relieved and after joining all of you on spring break, the kid sort of settles into the spare bunk in your son's room. Over the next couple of years, he becomes so integrated into your daily existence that the grandmother stops checking up on him.

The years roll by. You get formal guardianship over the kid, so you can enroll him in school and make medical decisions for him, but adoption is out of the question, as the mother, when she's not in custody somewhere, won't consent. You effectively raise him, send him off to college like your other kids, and generally consider him to be part of the family.

What happens if you die without a will?

He's a stranger to you, as far as the law is concerned. Not your intestate heir, that's for sure.

What about that trust for you and your "descendants" that your grandparents set up? The one that gives you a few grand a year of mad money and that you'd hoped the kids would use wisely after you're gone. You check that document, and it says, "Descendants shall mean lawful, blood descendants of the grantor," pretty common language in older trusts. It means only your own, non-adopted biological kids and grandkids, born in lawful marriages, are included. So, not this kid.

Geez, that's not fair—the kid really is part of the family now. So, you change your will and leave him a chunk of your estate, just to make sure he gets *something*, and right about a week before you die, he has a child out of wedlock with your daughter. What's everybody's status *now*?

Got a headache?

Well, the bad news is that the only sector of society that deals with *Non-Traditional Relationships* worse than politicians do, is the Law (which, not coincidentally, is usually written by politicians). By now, I've drilled into your head what a lousy deal intestacy is, how you should be ashamed of yourself if you die without a will, just to save a few bucks, and how the *choices* the Law makes for you are never those you'd make yourself. Nowhere is this truer than if your interpersonal relationships are ones not yet recognized, not yet officially sanctioned, or not yet even understood by the Law, the people who write it and the people who enforce it.

The laws governing intestate disposition of property at death basically make assumptions about what *most people* would want to happen to their stuff at their deaths. To make those assumptions, the law relies on three things: history, value judgments and human nature. With Non-Traditional Relationships, those not yet officially defined or recognized in the law, there isn't much history and you may not agree with the law's value judgments. The reason those intestacy statutes give everything to spouses and kids, or then more-distant relatives, is they *assume* that's what most people would want.

Those are considered the safe assumptions, the ones made by the legislators adopting these laws. Much as I respect legislators, they tend to be a conservative lot, folks often less on the cutting edge of social change than your kids and their friends.

What sorts of human interaction would be viewed as Non-Traditional under the law?

- Unmarried relationships between people of any sex or gender, if those people would like to be treated just like they're married.

- The kid I described at the opening of this chapter, who was raised by you and who you want considered just like a part of the family, whatever "part" that may be.

- The un-related kid you adopt as an adult, just because you couldn't get the parents to relinquish parental rights, or because you want the kid treated like a "descendant" under Uncle Harry's trust.

- Step children you think of just like they're your kids, even though, legally, they're not.

- The grandchild you adopt as your own child, because your druggy kid and her spouse can't raise the grandkid.

- Any child born out of legally-recognized wedlock.

- That child conceived with donor eggs or sperm, or incubated by a surrogate, in each case where you skimped on the cost, didn't get the lawyer I told you to get, so you screwed up the legalities of *that* relationship.

Until just a few years ago, this list would have included marriage between people of the same sex.

This list could go on endlessly, what with gender fluidity and sexual identity, and every day, the creative forces in the Universe conjure up new and complicated versions of what the law treats as *Unconventional or Non-Traditional*, but you get the idea.

I'm not here to pass judgment on folks creating or living in these situations: As far as I'm concerned, if you don't break any laws or hurt anybody, what you do in your spare time is your business. In forty years of practicing law, I've seen the pain and anguish folks in these relationships suffer at the hands of a dis-approving public. Unfortunately, the law is slow to recognize, then approve of, then sanction, and finally come up with *default rules*, to deal with these human interactions.

An example:

Even though a significant chunk of the American population is born outside of conventional marital relationships, until the Supreme Court buried the practice in 1976, children born of those relationships were generally not intestate heirs of their birth fathers—they would inherit nothing from their intestate fathers. While the justification for that heavy-handed bit of social engineering was often couched in terms of preventing fraudulent claims, it was really a form of value judgment by the powers-that-be. Even after the Supreme Court made such laws unconstitutional, states like Illinois, where I live, still didn't allow inheritance the other way—*from* deceased out-of-wedlock kids to their birth fathers, when the kids had money, usually from lawsuit recoveries. When out-of-wedlock kids with personal injury recoveries died, inheritance from those kids only went to the mothers and their other kids. The Illinois Supreme Court didn't kill that little chunk of moralizing—essentially punishing fathers for conceiving out-of-wedlock children, but not mothers—until the 1990's. The obvious basis for that rule: Of course, the "guilty" party in the perceived bad behavior that is un-wedlock impregnating, *is always the male.*

That's the way the law typically makes these rules—value-laden assumptions about right and wrong, not necessarily the way you would make them, if you were the referee.

So, now what?

If we're talking about what *you* want to do with *your* money, the solution is relatively easy, assuming you're willing to spend some money on a lawyer. While everybody should gleefully go to their probate lawyer and crank out a will, if you're somebody with an *Non-Traditional Relationship* in your orbit, you really, *really* need to do this. That's because you can give anything to a person you designate *by name*, as opposed to by class, like "my spouse" or "my descendants." In every state of the union, anybody can leave money to anybody in a will, subject to any conditions or qualifications, unless that gift violates *public policy.*

What's *that* mean? What it *doesn't* mean is a prohibition against giving money to folks in relationships once officially frowned upon, like same-sex partners or unmarried partners. The *public policy* restrictions all are aimed at discouraging you from using your money to entice outcomes that most people no longer find appropriate, such as:

"I give a hundred thousand dollars to my son Stanley, if he divorces that spouse Shelly, who I always hated." (Can't do this—encourages divorce, still considered a bad thing—the encouraging, not the divorcing).

"I give a hundred thousand dollars to my son Stanley, as long as he doesn't marry an Asian woman." (Can't do this—encourages discrimination).

"I give a hundred thousand dollars to my son Stanley, as long as he only marries somebody within the Zoroastrian Faith," (Increasingly, in many states, can't do this either—encourages discrimination by faith and restricts religious freedom).

Otherwise, you can swing away, as they say in baseball: As long as you are careful to provide for people with whom you share Non-Traditional Relationships *by name,* your gifts will be followed. There's no prohibition about the *who-gets-what* or the *under-what-circumstances* of giving, other than those public policy barriers. The key is not to rely on gifts to *people described with legal terms.* No, "My spouse"; no "My descendants"; no "My intestate heirs".

I even give this advice to people in same-sex marriages that are now legally sanctioned, because I always worry that a change in the make-up of government or the Supreme Court might result in a rollback of some of the more progressive laws that make same-sex relationships legally protected.

It's a tougher problem if you're talking about how to deal with people who you can't designate in your will by their proper names. What if you want the descendants of your child from her same-sex relationship, to get some of your dough if that child dies? "I leave the residue to Sally, but if she predeceases me, to her descendants," may not get the job done. Those kids, that both you and Sally think of as hers, may not be born yet, so you can't *name* them, and if they are born to her same-sex partner outside of a recognized marriage or in some artificial conception without Sally's biology, the law where you live might not consider the kids *as Sally's descendants.*

The only safe way to do this is to tell the lawyer drafting your will exactly what you want—who's to get money and who isn't—and under exactly what circumstances—married or not, biologically related or not. Coming up with sufficiently defined terms to cover your intentions is an evolving science with probate lawyers, and the only sure thing is to assume it's not fully worked out yet. And, as soon as the relationships seem so recognized in the law that the problem seems fixed, relationships evolve again. Take gender fluidity: No probate lawyer routinely considered the impact of transgender relationships on wills and trusts a short decade ago. So, you need to constantly customize your will, if you want to safely provide for people in these relationships.

You can give a child a *Power of Appointment*, the ability to redirect the gift you make to her, to anybody she desires. This leaves the choice to the next generation, in case your kids' families and intended beneficiaries are not settled by your death. The key is to be specific and name beneficiaries when you can, or explain under what circumstances you want unnamed persons to get something.

Otherwise:

No Will Means a Whole, New You

June and Ann have lived together for a decade. Each was married to male spouses before, but they're now divorced from their former spouses and in a same-sex relationship, without formal marriage. They've got no kids. Their nearest relatives are parents and siblings, with whom they have strained interactions because their families have never approved of their same-sex relationship.

Ann picks up what seems like a routine infection and is treated with an antibiotic, but one night she has an adverse reaction to the medication and dies in her sleep.

June, grief stricken, calls an ambulance, but the doctors at the hospital give her the bad news that Ann is D.O.A., so they need to release her body to a funeral director. When June tries to sign for the burial directions, the hospital staff tells her, Sorry, but the authorized signer must be next of kin or somebody designated in Ann's will.

Ann's got no will and June does not qualify as a "next-of-kin," at least, not on the form the nurse is reading, which lists conventional family ties like spouse, child or parent.

While June is scrambling, desperately calling her lawyer, Ann's parents, who June dutifully called to give them the bad news, are checking in with the hospital staff. Before June can even try to stop them, they've authorized the hospital to release Ann's body to a funeral home.

Ann's parents not only refused to acknowledge June and Ann's relationship—they *resented* it, blamed it for the break-up of Ann's conventional marriage—and steadfastly tried to deny the same-sex aspect of Ann's new life.

After trying unsuccessfully to influence the funeral arrangements, June reluctantly attends the open-casket wake Ann's parents have arranged. Her parents have mostly invited Ann's friends and relatives from Ann's "former" life. When June arrives at the funeral home, she is shocked by Ann's appearance in the open coffin. While living with June, Ann had become uncomfortable with her traditional, female gender role, stopped wearing makeup and dressed exclusively in button-down collar shirts and jeans.

June's angst arises because Ann's parents have outfitted Ann in the most conventionally feminine attire and get-up possible: They've put her in a long, blond Miss-America wig, dolled up her face with fake eyelashes, rouge and bright red lipstick, and dressed her in a formal, bridesmaid-looking gown, complete with plunging neckline.

When June approaches the coffin, she loses it. A scuffle breaks out, in which June and Ann's parents exchange blows, and as June falls on the coffin to embrace her former partner, it tumbles over and Ann's body slips out. The Funeral Director calls the cops and has them all arrested: It turns out, in the state where they live, it's a misdemeanor for anybody to, "Secret, disturb or otherwise interfere with a corpse prepared for burial." So, they all get charged and then get bonded out of jail. (As an aside, I am willing to bet all the money in my wallet that, whatever bad things any of them expected might result from not having a will, going to jail wasn't one of them).

The dispute goes to court, while Ann's body is put in the undertaker's fridge. Ultimately, June loses and Ann is buried in the country-singer get-up, one that probably has her spinning in her grave.

"Ann would have been mortified," June complains to her lawyer.

"It's unfortunate," her lawyer laments. "All she needed was a will, designating you executor and giving you the authority to make the funeral arrangements."

"Ann thought lawyers were all chumps—stooges to the power structure," June responds.

"Perhaps, but we're *your* stooges," lawyer adds, as he fills out the forms to refund June's bond.

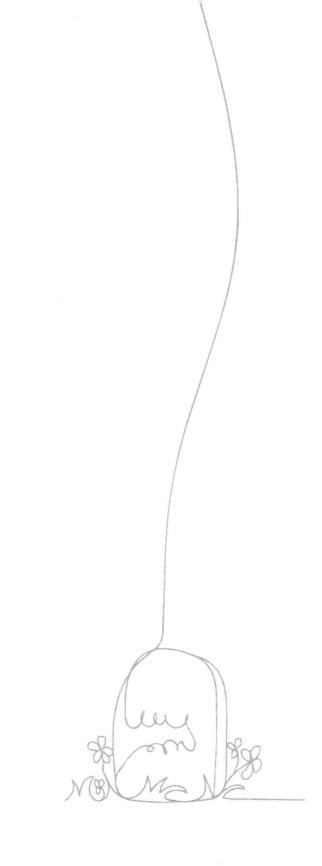

22. LOSING IT: YOU'RE GONNA DIE, BUT FIRST, YOU'RE GONNA FORGET YOUR CAR KEYS

I was born in 1954, and grew up in an Italian neighborhood. We lived, like most folks there, in a three-flat, a free-standing house with three stories and separate homes on each level. My grandparents lived on the top floor; my uncle and aunt, and, eventually, their kids, lived on the first; we lived in the middle. My grandparents did a lot of porch sitting, and their days consisted pretty much of asking anybody walking by two questions: "What are 'ya doing?" and "Where are 'ya going?" These were not innocent inquiries; the questions were asked with the utmost suspicion and the conviction that an honest answer would reveal criminal intent and illegal activity. It was a pretty oppressive environment, because if your answers were deemed unsatisfactory, there was a legitimate fear you might get brained by my grandmother, who carried a brick in her handbag.

The thing was: You couldn't get away with anything. The family lived in that arrangement until my grandparents died.

Fast forward to my first job at a law firm. It was 1978. In addition to handling clients' probate estates, I probated all the dead law partners and their spouses. My typical dead person in those days was a 55 to 68-year-old male smoker, with heart disease, lung disease, or both. Fifteen short years later, my typical dead person was a 63-year-old female with metastatic breast cancer.

By 1990, I was no longer probating three flats with extended families living inside. Grandma and grandpa were in extended care and nursing facilities, or, if they were lucky, they were living on their own.

What happened?

A number of things. Start with Ida May Fuller. You may justifiably ask, Who the *heck* is Ida May Fuller? Ms. Fuller, late of Ludlow, Vermont, was, on January 31, 1940, the very first recipient of a monthly retirement benefit check form the Social Security Administration—twenty-two dollars and fifty-four cents. I'd argue that $22.54 changed American culture more than television, birth control, marijuana or the assassination of JFK.

Social Security eventually gave elderly parents and grandparents a degree of independence. I grew up before this overspread the Country, climbing the back-porch stairs from the basement, where we had our only shower. I was naked except for a towel, with my hair dripping wet, and *each and every day,* my grandmother, who lived with us, asked me the same question: "Where you going?" (To rob a bank in the nude? Hit the racetrack wrapped in a towel?)

I bet that if you can't say you lived forever with your grandparents, it's in part because Social Security gave your old folks and grandfolks the ability to live on their own, instead of riding out their golden years in a sort of Old-World Family Co-Op.

What else happened to bring about this change in the way we grow old? There's public health: In 1965, when the U.S. had about 185 million people, over 42 percent of them, *80 million people,* smoked cigarettes. When you stop to consider that a large number of the non-smokers were babies and kids, you realize that a huge proportion of the adult population smoked. By 2010, that percentage had dropped by *over half,* to 19%. During the same period, average American life expectancies jumped, over four years for males and an astonishing six years for females. Even more amazing—life expectancies grew ten years for males and fifteen for females, if those people had money (Yes, they live longer).

These and other trends conspired to change an important aspect of the way we live, and equally important, the way we die. Zip back to my starting days as a probate lawyer in 1978: I worked in the largest county courthouse in the country, which serves millions of people. At that time, it had two probate courtrooms to deal with guardianship cases for disabled elderly folks, compared to seven courtrooms handling dead people's estates. Today, that same courthouse has only four courtrooms for dead people's estates, but six for guardianships for the elderly. And, inside that courthouse, I tried a case in 1981 that was all about an old guy with Alzheimer's Disease, who'd been ripped off as he started to lose it. The trial went on for weeks, and when I got the five-thousand-page trial transcript, the court reporter had typed "Old-Timer's Disease" each and every time somebody in the courtroom uttered the words, "Alzheimer's Disease". She really thought that's what people were saying: She'd never heard of Alzheimer's, a phenomenon that wouldn't happen today.

This upward trend in the number of people in guardianships has nothing to do with changes in the law: It's actually harder today to open up a guardianship proceeding than it was in 1978, and widespread use of those dreaded Powers of Attorney has also cut into the guardianship population. No, this trending is entirely demographic. People are living longer, living alone more often, and, much as we'd like to pretend this isn't happening, losing it more as they toddle off into old age.

While we'd all like to think that Gramps is fit and independent as he drives to the grocery store or as he administers his own medication, there's a whopping amount of medical evidence that important mental functions decline in *everybody* past age seventy, with some important skills going faster than others. Three cognitive abilities that are critical to sorting out money and not letting people rip you off, start to decline well before many others. They are:

- Executive Function
- Free Recall Memory; and
- Selective Attention

Executive Function is the ability to hatch a plan, take necessary steps and follow it through to completion, and then take stock of the results. For example: "I'm going to go see my probate lawyer today. I'll collect all my financial records, fill out that financial statement she sent me, map out the location of her office, check for public parking in the area, then call her and make an appointment. Better set my alarm—it'll take longer than my usual trip to the store, so I'll need to get up early......" Then, after the visit, "*Phew*, got that done, but my lawyer did say I needed to send her a copy of my old will before she can draft that new one, so I need to go to the bank and get it out of my safe deposit box, so I can copy it......"

Executive Function is one of the first things that starts to go as you sunset, and it is the first thing to completely flame out when you start getting Alzheimer's Disease—not short-term memory, as is widely believed.

Delayed Free Recall Memory means you're losing the ability to immediately retrieve stored information from memory without a cue or a hint. "Oh, there's *what's-his-name*?" is probably the best example. While that may happen to most of us at some time, it happens more often when you're over seventy. And, it happens with folks you should have no trouble identifying, like good friends, the kid who lives downstairs, the regular receptionist at the nursing home. This ability also starts to go quickly as you age.

Selective Attention is the ability to focus on specific and important information in your environment, while ignoring the unimportant stuff creeping into the scene. The best example is driving a car: When you're young, it's easy not to worry about the guy on the car radio, squawking on about which mini-mart has the best price for a six pack—you instinctively watch that woman pushing the baby carriage who's about to cross the street just ahead, and reflexively cover that brake pedal with the center of your foot, not the toe. Past age 70, it's not surprising to hear a back-seat driver, mumble, "Hey, look out for that baby carriage......" and you realize you were listening to that car radio. This ability, to automatically select out the important stuff from a sensory-overload world, also starts to slip by fast, even if you have no diagnoseable cognitive impairment associated with aging. It's one reason why older people are more easily distracted.

Then, there's age-related *Impairments*. Sad but true: More than half of all people over eighty actually have some form of cognitive impairment, such as cardio-vascular (Inadequate blood flow to the brain); ischemic (stroke); delirium (metabolic disorders like kidney impairment); or structural deterioration, like Alzheimer's Disease (essentially, invasive plaques in the brain). And, sorry, hate-mail be damned: Almost nobody over age 90 is fully cognitively intact.

Meanwhile, more and more of those older folks with slowly creeping deficiencies and impairments are living alone, or with another elderly companion, or with a paid attendant or care-giver. The collision of these trends leads to an alarming, escalating incidence of elder abuse, and more often than not, that manifests as financial abuse.

One more trend is aggravating the problem of elderly financial abuse. When my parents were living in that three-flat, not all that long ago, there was a reasonable likelihood that all their kids would stay in town: One would be a cop; one would work for a local business; one might work for the City, driving a garbage truck; and the one who managed to go to City College, she might teach in a local grade school. Everybody went to the same church on Sunday, and afterward they all went to one of those four-hour "lunches" put on by my grandmother. Nobody in the family had a leg up on anybody else, in the smarmy, ingratiate yourself with Grandma sweepstakes, and nobody could effectively isolate Grandma from anybody else, since Grandma was constantly in everybody's face ("It's only been a few hours. You're *leaving*? You're not *hungry?*").

Today, adult kids from the snowy Midwest who can get out and still earn a living, do get out—they head to the coasts, where there are three important incentives for the move: They are, in order: 1. The weather's better; 2. The weather's better; and 3. The weather's better. There's also an element of what we used to call *Chaa-Chaa-Chaa* out on the coasts, that appears to be lacking in Pinkneyville, Iowa. In the Midwest, we call these relocated folks members of *Bi-Coastal Families*, since everybody's now in New York or California, unless they've moved to Vegas or Texas. This phenomenon doesn't even begin to address the other aspect of young-people flight: Corporate relocation victims, the folks that move every few months or years, whenever their boss at Integrated Electric Chair and Semi-Conductor™ decides they're needed in the Chattanooga plant.

The thing is, isolation of Mom and Pop is only half the problem. There's always somebody left behind—the younger brother who actually ended up driving that garbage truck for the city, or the perfectly content baby sister, who teaches at the local grade school. Two things always happen in these situations: First, that baby sister becomes the favored kid, who visits elderly mom, gets the Power of Attorney, and gets a bigger share under mom's new will. And, if she's a little unscrupulous, baby sis starts to get a lot of "gifts", from mom's accounts, to help her maintain her own lifestyle. Second, all those jet-setting, bi-coastal siblings fly into *outrage* when they find out about baby sister's favored treatment by elderly mom. This, baby sister will argue, even though they haven't seen mom in five years.

If I took on every case of financial exploitation where I got a call about somebody's elderly mom or dad, usually from the outraged out-of-towners who want baby sister's treachery undone, I could do nothing else, non-stop, every day of the year. So, since your mom, dad or grandparent may well become a victim, here's a bit of bad news for you Bi-Coasters and other out-of-towners: The last, legitimate baby-sister-isolated-and-ripped-off-elderly-dad case I observed, ended in protracted settlement discussions conducted by a retiring probate judge. In that case, there was no question that most of the hundreds of thousands collected by only-kid-in-town, had been illegally swiped after dad had lost his marbles. Offensive as that was, the Judge, himself a slightly younger member of Dad's generation, openly expressed sympathy with stay-in-town daughter, and some intense lack of regard for those Bi-Coastal siblings. Sure, he felt *obligated* to acknowledge all the laws that make elder abuse both a crime and a civil wrong answerable in treble damages—but there was no disguising his bias in favor of stay-in-town baby sister.

And then, there's the rising epidemic of paid-or-unpaid-caregiver financial abuse. Right behind the stay-in-town sibling cases, comes the overly-friendly nurse, step-daughter or companion, paid to take care of dad or mom, who miraculously ends up the main beneficiary under the new will (drafted by a lawyer selected by the caregiver), or who suddenly is on the deed to dad's house, or has her family's living expenses heavily subsidized by mom's credit cards. This has become such a recurring problem that many states have added laws to the books that declare these gifts and transfers to paid caregivers fraudulent *as a matter of law*. Sorry, no chance for caregiver to go to court and argue, "Mrs. Smith *really, really* loved me and my kids more than her own Bi-Coastal, out-of-the-picture kids and grandkids."

Ironically, the same laws sometime contain a presumed gift, or *Custodial Claim*, of hundreds of thousands *In favor of* a child or other relative of mom who becomes elderly mom's caretaker. Do we see a pattern developing? Even the state legislature discriminates against out-of-towners and in favor of the stay-at-home sibling.

I can just hear you grumbling about how this impinges on your lifestyle, be it out-of-town jet setter, too busy to act as glorified caregiver for mom, or independent grandma, who *likes* not having your kids and grandkids up your nose all the time. That's fine, but the forces that create elder abuse opportunities aren't going to change. Multi-national corporate employers are not going to stop moving employees around like chess pieces, and kids with portable money and employment skills are not going to tough out the rest of their lives in snowy Bumpersticker, North Dakota, just to keep an eye out for elderly mom.

There is a solution to this problem. It's in the hands of every person over the age of sixty, and it's relatively inexpensive.

And, you're going to be *shocked* to learn that this solution involves going to see your probate lawyer. Wait—even more shocking—it requires going to see your probate lawyer *often*.

If, like me, you started regularly seeing your doctor once a year when you passed age sixty, and dutifully pay for those exams that usually yield nothing more than, "Here, pee in this cup," and, "You should lose some weight and reduce your stress levels," you shouldn't be offended when I tell you that you need to start doing the same thing with your probate lawyer. Stop by once a year, whether you think you need it or not. Yes, the several-hundred-dollar bill you'll get every year is annoying, but it's peanuts compared to the cost of untangling the financial consequences of elder abuse.

While your probate lawyer is no doctor, they've probably become adept at sensing declines in your capacity, particularly those that impact your ability to manage money and resist financial exploitation. Many probate lawyers will even screen you with armchair cognitive capacity evaluations, like the Mini Mental Status Exam, which can be conducted sitting in a chair in your lawyer's office, without electrodes strapped to your head or needles poked in your arms. A qualified probate lawyer will be able to tell if you're a potential victim in the making.

What can lawyers do? Most probate lawyers will have contacts with legitimate service providers who can both monitor your care and, if needed, provide you with new caregivers for oversight. If you consent, they can notify *all* your kids or other close family members. The more people know about your cognitive status, the less likely any one person, be it trusted son or loyal caregiver, can accomplish a rip-off. Most importantly, your lawyer can help you transfer your assets into a funded, revocable trust and hook you up with the trust department at your local bank, to manage that trust for you.

I know, I know—those bank trust departments charge fees and you've heard that their investment results never made anybody into the next Warren Buffett. Get over it; that's not their job. First Local Community Bank, or, if your account is big enough, one of the major banks, act as your co-trustee to protect you and your money, not turn you into a late-in-life tech billionaire. They can pay your bills, get your taxes done, find a safe place to park your money, and most importantly, sense trouble early on, if they see suspicious activity in your charge account or unauthorized money movement. I've been working with bank folks like this for decades and never once seen a crook or even a stooge in the ranks. If they do something aggressively stupid and lose your money on bad investments, they usually step up and cover the losses. The fee is modest, compared to the service provided.

And, my favorite aspect of funding your revocable trust is the hidden security value of having a bank act as co-trustee with you. How's that work? You can state in the trust document that any amendment or *revocation* (cancelling the trust or ripping large sums of money out of it) can only be done on the signature of *both* you *and* the Bank. No fraudster, be it your adult kid or your caregiver, realizes that the document they slipped in front of you to sign will be ineffective without the Bank's signature, whether it's a crooked trust amendment or even a bank account withdrawal statement. If the Bank is your co-trustee, you still have control (you can remove the bank as long as you're competent) but changes and money withdrawals are only effective with the co-signature of a bank officer. And, it won't help those scoundrels to buy this book, read all the way to page hundred and something, and proclaim: "Ah-hah! I'll just get the Bank to sign off," because those bank officers are trained to sniff out this stuff, so *they won't sign.*

Does it seem like I'm overreacting?

The Bi-Coastal Family Gets a Geography Lesson

Ted's kids are all successful, go-getter types, so they've all left the snowy Midwest for exotic places with coastlines and super-high real estate taxes, all except daughter Gina. Ted's retired, living in the rambling, four-bedroom house the kids grew up in, and is quietly managing the million-dollar nest egg he accumulated working forty years as a salesman at a local office products company. His spouse has been dead for a decade, and he spends his days working as a volunteer at the local library and hitting golf balls at the nearby driving range. Gina looks in on him, once a week.

Ted hasn't seen his lawyer in years, figures, *who needs that guy,* and anyway, he's got an old will that divides his estate evenly between his four kids, three of whom pop back into town for the holidays. They all seem to get along.

Ted ran into a guy in the check-out line at the grocery store a few months ago, somebody with a bow tie and nice shoes, and the guy chatted him up on the way out the door. Turns out the guy, Pete, works for his own little accounting place, Pete's Perfect Performance, a small shop with an office up above the massage parlor in the local strip-mall next to the grocery store.

Pete convinces Ted to let him manage some of the million-dollar nest egg, and soon Pete is reporting *remarkable* returns, small sums doubling almost monthly ("*If we could only do this with a little more money, think of the leverage*", Pete proclaims). Pretty soon, Ted gives Pete a lot more, then most of the nest egg, to manage. Something for nothing always seems like a good deal, Ted figures, since Pete doesn't charge fees for achieving these impressive results ("I get paid off the *leverage,*" says Pete).

Ted's getting tired and forgetful, so he gives up golf. When he tells his son Rocky about this, Rocky asks Gina about Ted. Gina says, "Hmmm, he seems OK to me."

Rocky's not convinced—Ted *loved* golf—so Rocky makes a trip back into town to visit Ted. There, he sees the statements from "Pete's Perfect Performance, Inc.," and notices they look hand-typed.

"Dad, who *is* this guy?" Rocky asks.

"A *genius,*" Ted announces.

Rocky goes to visit Pete and can't get very good answers to any of his questions, so he goes to Ted's old lawyer, to check out Pete and his company.

"Don't know him, and I can't find this "Perfect Performance" place registered with the Securities and Exchange Commission," lawyer says. "Then, you better check him out," Rocky decides.

When the lawyer confronts Pete, Pete produces some home-made stock certificates showing that most of Ted's money has been invested in "Pete's Perfect Performance, Inc.," of which Ted is now the largest single investor—in fact, he owns a bigger stake in the oper-ation than Pete. When Rocky and the lawyer ask Ted about this, he admits he "signed a bunch of stuff," but can't honestly say he had any idea he was investing directly in Pete's business, effectively support-ing Pete and his lifestyle.

While the SEC is busy raiding Pete's operation, the financial records they turn over to Rocky and Ted show that all Ted's money essentially accomplished was to pay Pete's salary and office expenses. The SEC sets up a victim's fund in which Ted becomes the single biggest claimant, and as they haul Pete off to jail, this brings about a serious reckoning meeting between Rocky, Ted and Ted's lawyer.

"Well, Dad, at least you've got the equity in your house, to tide you over until they recover something from that dirt-bag Pete," remarks Rocky, who genuinely does not want to give Ted this last bit of bad news. "But, you're gonna need to sell the place and move to an apartment—"

"Uhhh, about that," lawyer interrupts. "I pulled a title report on the house, and it looks like a year ago, Dad signed a deed giving the house to Gina."

"I did?" Dad asks, shaking his head. "She said that was some form for the State, something to reduce the taxes on the place."

"Well, it reduced *your* real estate taxes, because you don't own it anymore," lawyer remarks.

The litigation to set aside the transfer of Ted's house to daughter Gina ("I was always Dad's *favorite,* and he *wanted* this....") goes on longer than the SEC proceedings against Pete and Perfect Performance. While Rocky gets the deed to Gina tossed out, most of Ted's money is gone, and when the SEC wraps up the victim's fund, Ted gets $195.00 and a certificate for future proceeds, once Pete is out of jail and works off his restitution plea bargain.

They all go to the lawyer to pick up the check. "The last time Ted came to see me," lawyer tells Rocky, "It was years ago. I tried to get him to put everything in trust and have Community Trust & Savings take it over, but he didn't like their fee schedule."

Ted, who's staring off into space and overhears this, responds, "You *bet* I didn't like their fees—it was a real rip off."

"Dad—" Rocky starts in, but Ted interrupts.

"That Pete didn't charge *any fees....*"

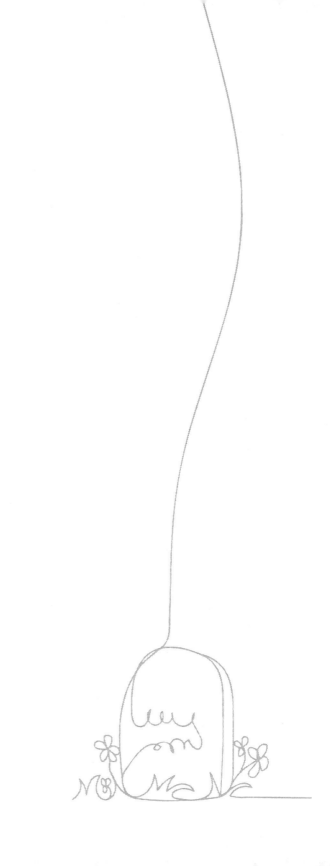

23. FINDING A LAWYER: WHERE TO GO AND HOW MUCH TO PAY?

Now that I've nagged you into opening your wallet and seeking out legal help, where do you go to find a lawyer? Like a lot of things in America today, that's largely a function of your Zip Code. Most major metropolitan areas have a Bar Association tethered to the largest city in the area, and typically, they offer very good (and free) lawyer referral services. In Chicago, the web address is Https://lrs.chicagobar.org. In New York City, it's https://www.nycbar.org/get-legal-help/. In Los Angeles, it's https://www.lacba.org/need-legal-help. I know those three only cover ten percent of the U.S. population, but if I can effectively use a search engine, anybody can. If you generally search the terms "[City name]" and then "bar association", you should find the service in your area. There are also several privately-operated attorney search websites, although I'd start with the local bar associations first and go private if you don't find what you need.

These bar organizations may not be the best differentiators of service quality and know-how, but the folks on their lists will be people who can do the work and won't be recently disbarred for frequent intoxication or stealing clients' money.

If you're in Buford, Wyoming (Pop. 1), it's a little tougher to find somebody who can draft your will. If you have an accountant, most work closely with probate lawyers, so ask your accountant. If that doesn't work, every city in this country is in a county, and every county has a County Seat, the city within the county where the courthouse is located. In smaller, less populated locations, try calling the Clerk of the Court in the county courthouse. Even if there's no dedicated Probate Judge, the Clerk will at least be able to tell you where to find local lawyers, who all appear at their courthouse and regularly file probate cases.

It's always tough to know if your financial profile is too big or too small for a given lawyer, but a few things generally hold true:

- If you have millions, you need heavy-duty tax advice. The local guy in your neighborhood who is drawing up real estate contracts and handling DUI's, is probably not the best choice. And, the bar association services don't draw this distinction in handing out names. Even if you're not in a major metropolitan area, you need a lawyer who is in a decent-sized city. Sorry, sounds elitist, but that's where most of those lawyers work. Straight-forward online searching of law firms will probably get you to several decent choices. Make sure you are searching "Estate Planning" or "Private Client" or "Estates and Trusts" on law-firm websites, to find the folks who do this work for a living. Many big firms will have groups who specialize in estate and death planning.

- If you don't have millions, and you just need asset planning and wills and trusts, your local people who pop up on those Bar Association referral searches will most likely be able to handle your case, and will likely not charge an arm and a leg for the service.

- If you're looking for people who've effectively been through a legitimate review process, ACTEC, the American College of Trust and Estate Counsel, is an indispensable organization (Full disclosure; I'm a long-time member, but don't let that scare you—they don't pay me, I pay them dues, and I get no discount for this endorsement). ACTEC attorneys all specialize in estate and trust service, have worked in the field a minimum of ten years and write and speak on the subject, so they should be up to snuff. To get into ACTEC, attorneys needed to pass local and nationwide membership votes, so a gas-bag who doesn't know his or her stuff won't be a member. ACTEC's website has a search tool, www.actec. org/fellows/directory , which will locate active members in your geographical area. Many of them may be higher octane than you need. If that's the case, they usually know the general practitioners in their area, and can make a better, more informed cross-referral for you than the typical bar association.

So, ignore your loud-mouthed, drunken neighbor, rambling on about how all lawyers are crooks, and contact one of these outfits.

Things to expect:

- You'll need to do a lot of the work yourself. A complete listing of your assets and debts is a critical first step, and the more detailed a list you prepare, the less time the lawyer needs to spend digging out this information.

- If you already have wills and trusts, make sure to send them on to the lawyer ahead of time. It will help the lawyer focus on existing biographical information and prior planning that may need revamping.

- If you're married or divorced, be sure to provide the lawyer with any pre-nuptial or post-nuptial agreements, as well as any divorce decrees. You may have obligations under those agreements and divorce documents that need to be addressed in your wills and trusts.

- Make sure to collect from your employer lists of any pension, profit-sharing or other employee benefit plans or insurance you have through your employment, and copies of any existing beneficiary designations for those plans.

- Same thing for existing, non-work insurance policies. Copies of the policies and beneficiary designations are important to provide ahead of time.

- If anybody in your family, particularly a spouse, is not *both* a citizen *and* full-time resident of the U.S., be sure to have complete immigration and work status information available.

On the other hand, be careful if:

- The attorney does not ask you for asset and liability information, or give you a biographical and asset worksheet to fill out.

- The attorney can't or won't tell you up front what the entire legal planning engagement is likely to cost. There are always exceptions—particularly for people who can't make up their minds, have non-traditional family relationships or complex asset holdings and ownership. Still, the attorney should be able to tell you what the standard charge looks like.

- The attorney doesn't offer you an engagement letter, or at least make clear if he or she is just representing you, you and your spouse, or anybody else associated with your family or your plan.

- The attorney makes suggestions about specific charities to write into your wills and trusts. If that happens, be sure to ask if the attorney has any relationship to that charity, like being on the board of the charity or even representing the charity. These conflicts should always be disclosed.

- The attorney suggests you name him or her as executor or trustee, or agrees to that suggestion if it comes from you. This is always an inherent conflict of interest, even if it is the right choice in a given case. Remember, there's always a local bank that can take the job, and they're not drafting your will and placing themselves into a money-making position.

And, if the attorney suggests you include a gift to him or her under the will or trust (this happens), get up and walk out. Get a new lawyer.

Most lawyers charge by the hour and people in big cities charge more per hour than people in small towns and rural areas. The more complicated your plan and your needs, the more it is going to cost. These days, some attorneys are willing to offer fixed-fee deals, where your bill is capped unless something unexpected creeps in. Be careful, though—sometimes these fixed fees are priced to out-cost the hourly service. You're not always better off with one of these deals, so think twice about a fixed-fee deal.

The most important advice is the refrain I've been drumming into your head for the last twenty-two chapters—don't be penny-wise and pound-foolish about paying for skilled, informed help. Cutting corners will come back to bite you, or, more likely, your heirs, families and friends who need to clean up the mess you leave behind from do-it-your-selfing and general penny pinching.

I can just see you smirking—some people *never* learn, so, absorb this:

The Scam, The Lawsuit, The Riot, The Fist Fight, But Almost No Legal Fees

So, there's this Guy—a retirement home developer who runs his own business, developing entire communities for retirees, the kind of stuff carved out of farmers' fields when urban sprawl begins to encroach and the elderly residents start looking for an alternative to nursing homes.

One of his projects is to develop a semi-private golf course and surrounding retirement "village", in an area beginning to see the nibbling of population growth on the peripheral borders of a growing suburban expansion. It's an area with a few small lakes and rolling countryside that will need some meaningful grading and development.

The Guy's getting old, doesn't want to do the hard stuff himself, so he's looking for somebody young and aggressive to undertake the project. He's approached by a couple of go-getters, the kind of people with big ideas but no money of their own to put into the project. He likes their aggressiveness, so he decides he'll finance the project by borrowing on the farmland, then loaning the go-getters the money they'll need. He'll take out a mortgage on several hundred acres of the farmland he's just bought.

The Guy is old school, hates lawyers and hates paying lawyer's bills, so he goes online and buys a bunch of pre-printed legal forms. By the time he's done putting the deal together, he's filled out a bunch of those forms, forms he assumes will give him his money back sooner rather than later. Those forms actually give his young retirement village salesmen a lot of power to do stuff with the property. He's checked a lot of little boxes on the forms, and one of those boxes gives these young hipsters something called, "Debtor in Possession" rights, which means they get to do what they want with the property, even if the project is in trouble, even though they have no money in the deal and even though they haven't yet paid him a penny. Yeah, he probably should not have checked *that* box.

Turns out these sub-developers are more than just aggressive. As they've built the clubhouse, landscaped the golf courses and built private residences around one of the lakes, they've racked up monstrous additional debt. And, the memberships aren't selling: The place is still too far away from homes to attract much interest. No problem—they've got a new plan—*Condo the place*. That always seems to work in the do-it-yourself, become-a-real-estate-developer self-help classes at the local motel out by the Interstate. So, they begin "selling" lots around the lake with the private residences that will give folks a view of the lake and free lifetime golf privileges.

One problem, though—there are no separate lots to sell, and the land can't be subdivided while it's subject to that humungous mortgage used to raise the development money in the first place. These guys are *creative*, and who needs all that formality anyway—they just print certificates for the lots they're selling, and they sell away those phony lots.

Meanwhile, our Guy, Mr. Property Owner, has no idea this is all going on and only slightly more idea how much power he's given these con men in those do-it-yourself legal documents he's drafted. He's just starting to get antsy because Go-Getter, Con-Job Guys haven't been paying down any of *his* mortgage, and the bankers are starting to ask questions.

Fortunately for this Guy, he dies. His son inherits this mess, right about the time that some of the owners of these worthless residence certificates start hiring lawyers, who begin asking serious questions for which there are no answers.

A very high-profile fraud lawsuit is filed in the local courts out by the new development and in a low-density population county, the suit is big news. Estate of Dead Guy gets sued too, and son hires an experienced Probate Litigator to try to straighten out the mess.

When they get to court, there's a mob outside the courtroom. Angry people swindled out of money for "shares" in the new retirement community they now know don't really exist, are shouting at everybody entering and leaving the courtroom. A fight breaks out and both Son, who had absolutely nothing to do with any of this, and his Probate Lawyer, who had even less to do with it, are punched out by people in the angry mob. To add insult to injury, the reporters take some pictures and the local paper runs a story featuring these photos, so that it appears like Son and Probate Lawyer are perps in this huge fraud. Their images are plastered all over local media.

Meanwhile, the Judge appoints a Bank to take over the entire project and the Bankers start unravelling the mess, selling off the land and paying back those consumers who got fleeced. There won't be much money left for Dead Guy's estate, but Son still needs to pay Probate Lawyer, who's keeping Son personally out of the firing lines.

When it's all over, Probate Lawyer gives Son a legal bill. It's not important exactly how big that bill is. For my purposes, it's just important to note that the legal bill is significantly, much, much more than five thousand dollars.

Son looks at the bill, snarls in disgust and says, "This fee is *outrageous.* You know, in his entire *life,* my Father *never* spent more than five thousand dollars on lawyers."

Thinking about the courtroom riot and getting punched in the nose, and about the millions of dollars Dead Guy lost in the deal, Probate Lawyer says to Son, "Well, I believe *that.*"